DISABILITY, CULTURE, AND EQU
Alfredo J. Artiles and Elizabeth B. Kozles

(Un)Learning Disability:
Recognizing and Changing Restrictive Views of Student Ability
ANNMARIE D. BAINES

Ability, Equity, and Culture:
Sustaining Inclusive Urban Education Reform
ELIZABETH B. KOZLESKI & KATHLEEN KING THORIUS, EDS.

Condition Critical—Key Principles for Equitable and Inclusive Education
DIANA LAWRENCE-BROWN & MARA SAPON-SHEVIN

(Un)Learning Disability

Disability

Recognizing and Changing
Restrictive Views
of Student Ability

AnnMarie D. Baines

Foreword by Ray McDermott

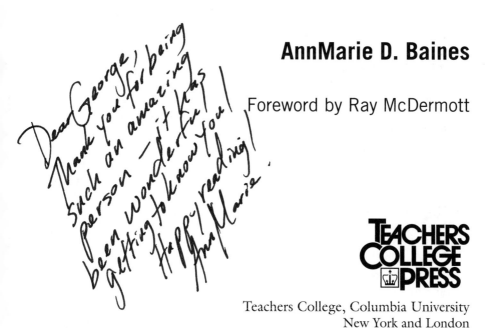

Dear George,
Thank you for being
such an amazing
person — it has
been wonderful
getting to know you!
Happy reading!
AnnMarie

TEACHERS
COLLEGE
PRESS

Teachers College, Columbia University
New York and London

Published by Teachers College Press, 1234 Amsterdam Avenue, New York, NY 10027

The research reported in this book was supported in part by a Science of Learning Center grant from the National Science Foundation to the LIFE Center and a Presidential Fellowship from the GO-MAP, both awarded by the University of Washington.

Library of Congress Cataloging-in-Publication Data

Baines, AnnMarie Darrow
    (Un)learning disability : recognizing and changing restrictive views of student ability / Annmarie D. Baines.
    pages cm.—(Disability, culture, and equity series)
    Includes bibliographical references and index.
    ISBN 978-0-8077-5536-5 (pbk.)—ISBN 978-0-8077-5515-0 (hardcover)
    ISBN 978-0-8077-7272-0 (ebook)
    1. Students with disabilities—Education. 2. Students with disabilities—
Psychology. 3. Youth with mental disabilities—Education. 4. Youth with
mental disabilities—Psychology. I. Title. II. Title: Unlearning disability. III.
Title: Learning disability.
    LC213.B35 2014
    371.9—dc23
                                                                2013044808

ISBN 978-0-8077-5536-5 (paper)
ISBN 978-0-8077-5515-0 (hardcover)
eISBN 978-0-8077-7272-0 (ebook)

Printed on acid-free paper
Manufactured in the United States of America

21 20 19 18 17 16 15 14   8 7 6 5 4 3 2 1

To the students, families, and educators
who welcomed me into their lives,
To Aurora, Adela and Steven Darrow,
who inspired my questions,
And to Paul Baines,
who always knew what I was trying to say
and loved me through it all.

Contents

Foreword

AnnMarie Baines brings us good news. She gives us reason to believe that millions of disabled children in American schools are in much better shape than their labels imply. With her multilayered look into the lives of eight teenagers labeled as LD, she tells of a boy diagnosed with Asperger's who becomes a recognized debate champion, a girl diagnosed with a language processing disorder who pushes schoolwork aside to write three novels in her own fashion, and another boy once diagnosed as autistic who spent his time whether in school or out having to be the best at everything he was asked to do. Her important news is that no one should ever give up on children, no matter difficult or even broken they seem, before engaging them as guides to new designs for learning and new sources of critique of what their adults have offered them.

Her portraits deliver bad news as well. As schools have narrowed down what counts as knowledge, teachers have been forced to attend more to test scores than to children in their care, and teenagers have had to create alternative pathways through the system: pathways often brilliant, sometimes dangerous, occasionally productive, but each in its way responsive to the pressures and contradictions of American education. The bad news is that failure—well documented and justified failure—is part of what schools produce, and LD has become a player in the competitive market of measured learning and degree granting.

For Baines, children are not just LD, as much as they are acquired by and must report to the social institution called LD. Whatever the potentials of their heads, hearts, or hands, they must put them to work in environments filled with diagnostic protocols, competitive tests, ideologies of inherent aptitude and intelligence, and attitudes about kinds of people by race and class. LD hangs out in a tough crowd.

More than a century ago, when my father couldn't sit still in his first grade classroom, a nun used his belt to tie him to a chair. Nine years later, he was delighted to leave school, and for the next 70 years, he resisted the odds and raised a large successful family. He never missed a moment of responsibility. Did he have to be tied to his chair? Of course not. Adults should never be mean to a child, and schools should never be occasions for cruelty. Parents should have resisted, and teachers should have raged against the conditions that invited tying a child to a chair.

Enter the LD movement of the 1960s, which promised a softening in how children who read too slowly or move too quickly for life in a traditional classroom can be understood and appreciated. For a moment, LD was a great idea. Then it became a social institution manipulated to various ends. Who could have predicted that parents who fought in the 1950s to get their children in special classes would insist on mainstreaming 20 years later; that minority parents would sue school systems to have their children tested and labeled; that a famous private school (serving wealthy parents and children with an average IQ of 137) felt the need to presort its children until, unbelievably and ridiculously, the measures had 60% of them "at risk"; or that well-to-do parents would pay for private testing to get their children labeled and thereby eligible for extra time on tests. LD labels perform to cultural neuroses and market conditions.

LD might still be a good idea, but now possesses a questionable history and an uncertain future. LD labels have acquired far too many children and have been used too often to downgrade and degrade rather than to upgrade those in need of a helping hand. LD labels have become a mainstay for salary lines and fitted to the strategic struggles over how the next generation is to replicate socioeconomic status of its previous generation.

To the good news (children are more able and interesting than their adults know) and bad news (schools live on invidious comparisons), let's add some irony. The very LD movement that promised to make learning in school safer has given schools new tools to make things worse. This is not as anyone planned or hoped for, but in a not unusual fashion, when people are called on to solve social problems, they imagine solutions conditioned by the same categories and practices within which the problems emerged.

AnnMarie Baines has been using her good news to confront the irony of educators working against our children while trying to make things better. In her fieldwork, she took an active role. She engaged the children in settings that enabled them to make the most of what they could do. She engaged them primarily in debate contests in which they had to show off what they know and what they can say well under conditions of public risk. She gave them a sense of purpose and conditions under which they could imagine growth and progress. As her profiles accumulate, she generalizes that the "students have a tendency to gravitate to where they feel like they can make a difference, transform others and themselves, and be appreciated by those who can exert control in their lives." A century of learning theory of all kinds—Dewey, Vygotsky, Lewin, Skinner, Bruner, and Cole—would agree, although it is not easy to deliver the right conditions in classrooms. The children are not the problem. In the right circumstances, they can handle fear and stress. They can handle failure. They can handle identity struggles. They can be relentless in pursuit of things getting better, and they are articulate about how they can prosper under situations beyond the classroom. The students recorded in this book are unanimous in celebrating what they can do in situations beyond the albatross LD labels they are forced to wear and bear in school. By their work, we can know them, and by their work, we can gain a critique of how we have allowed LD to make their situation more difficult. LD can be "unlearned."

AnnMarie Baines shows us how LD can be rephrased, readdressed, and reworked. LD can be a good idea again, but the labels have to be tied to conditions of growth, identity enhancement, and institutional change.

—Ray McDermott

Acknowledgments

Exploring human assumptions is frightening at times, especially when the process inevitably involves questioning one's own personal understandings along the way. I am deeply grateful to the students in this study, who not only allowed me to witness the experiences influencing their identities but also played an integral role in shaping mine. While they started out as research participants, the young people and families in this book have become my friends and family. To say that they have challenged my preconceptions is a glaring understatement—they have transformed my life and values by opening my eyes to lives more complex than I ever could have imagined. I will forever draw inspiration from the spirit, courage, generosity, and strength they showed me over the course of writing this book and beyond. I greatly appreciate everything you have done for me and I am so proud to know all of you.

While it is one thing to observe the experiences of others, it is another thing entirely to make meaning of them. I have been lucky to have had several important mentors on my personal pathway, who not only opened my eyes to new ways of looking at established phenomena, but also reminded me constantly of its value. To my coadvisor Charles "Cap" Peck: You made this work happen. From believing in the project to begin with, to finding the right connections to make the fieldwork a reality, to maintaining the perfect balance between questioning and encouragement, you always reminded me of the human dimension of research. To my coadvisor Philip Bell: I am indebted to you for your efforts to support this research. Thank you for teaching me not only how to document the stories of such incredible young people, but how to make their voices heard in a wide range of audiences that cut across conceptual boundaries. And to Ray McDermott: Thank you for your willingness to grab a cup of coffee with a graduate student you had never met. While your written work has had a profound impact on my thinking, I am grateful for the pleasure and privilege of our continued conversations and your mentorship. Your interactions with and treatment of others dismantle hierarchies every day, and I can only aspire to someday be able to do the same. My heartfelt thanks also go out to Susan Nolen, Patricia Wasley, and Sapna Cheryan for encouraging this work and informing my thinking every step of the way.

I owe a great deal to the schools and teachers* who took part in the study, along with the hard work of my research team—Aurora Darrow, LouAnn Lyon, Giovanna Scalone, Megan Huckabay, and Martin Reimer. Thanks go to Natalio Avani and my colleagues at San Francisco State for helping me continue this work. At the University of Washington, I thank Nancy Price, the Learning in Informal and Formal Environments (LIFE) Center, and the Graduate Opportunities for Minority Achievement Program (GO-MAP) for their endless support. At Teachers College Press, I am grateful to the dedication of Brian Ellerbeck, Alfredo Artiles, Elizabeth Kozleski, external reviewers, and the entire editing and production team for their careful critiques.

I have been blessed with an entire community of supporters whose love and confidence have inspired my endeavors. To my parents, Adela and Steven Darrow, I love you and I am deeply thankful for all of your encouragement, personal sacrifices, and wisdom that taught me how to dream and care for others. To my sister, Aurora Darrow: You inspire me with your strength, talent, and ability to go above and beyond. I could not have done this work without you. To my grandmother, Marianne Darrow, and mother-in-law, Helen Baines, thank you for giving me love and encouragement. My dear friends, Alison Marti, Sylvia Sudat, Shelli Bueno, and Audrey McIntyre—thank you for believing in me, keeping me sane, and being so patient, not to mention reading drafts and talking me through tricky details. I couldn't have asked for better friends. My deepest gratitude goes out to Jack McCauley, Tom Hehir, and Catherine and Sanford Berman—whose work inspired the broader lessons of this book—and the students I taught in Boston who kept me grounded in the realities they faced each day. I am thankful for the supportive community who helped realize this vision: Matt Falgares, Neoma Kenwood, Michele Harrison, Leslie, Simon, and the Cohen Family, Mariana Castro, Suzanna Tran, Tiffany Shem, Jeff and Karen Reimer, Eric and the Imhof Family, Davonte Akpan, Reesha Reed, Rebecca Dao, Kristy Tran, Margaret Spencer, Emily and Todd Groves, Emily Specter, Brennden and Patricia Ogura, Jonathan and David Frankel, Darrell and Sadaf Kinney, Andre Shie, Sierra and Julie Lee, Stephanie Lipscomb, Heather Snookal, Cristy Resendiz, Maddie Berger, Ardalan Terman, Peter and Shohreh Terman, Dori Goldberg, Tori Johnson, James Geiszler, Bernadette Bascom, Holly Call, and Colin Stapleton. My sincerest apologies to anyone I have forgotten, and know that I value your support.

Even with such a strong moral, social, and intellectual network, I could not have even begun to do this work without my brilliant and patient husband, Paul Baines. As busy as he was with his own academic endeavors, he was always an enduring sounding board for all of my questions and ideas, and often knew how to express my thoughts and concerns even better than I ever could. I am forever grateful for his intellectual assistance, ability to listen, clarity of mind, and love, every step of the way. Thank you for everything.

---

*All school, teacher, and student names used in the text are pseudonyms.

Educational Positioning and the Damage to Youth Potential

I'm right and you're wrong, I'm big and you're small, and there's nothing you can do about it.

—Roald Dahl, *Matilda*

Thirteen-year-old Tinsley Hawkins was hiding in a closet. From 4th grade, she regularly would come home from school and lock herself in her bedroom closet, or else she would curl up in a fetal ball on the floor and lie there. Her mother remembers, "School was extremely frustrating for her. She worked very hard and she could see that she was struggling and way behind the other kids. She felt very stupid, and in 4th grade things fell apart." Tinsley wasn't upset about her closet, though. "I like it in there," she says with a smile. "It's safer than school and you can just imagine things and no one tells you that you failed."

James Ovill used to like school. Or at least he liked kindergarten. His father remembers one day in 1st grade when James was particularly anxious about going into school because he didn't know how to do the work his teacher had assigned him the day before. "I remember him just sobbing," his father reflects. "He kept saying, 'I won't be forgiven.' That's pretty heart-breaking for a 6-year-old boy to say. That was a bad year and a bad introduction to school for him."

There was Devin Foster, whose teacher told him he "wasn't smart enough for her class," and Spencer MacArthur, whose peers said, "just didn't want to learn." There was Anthony Gustafson, who stopped participating when his elementary school teachers would ask, "Does anyone else have anything to say?" Anthony's mother looks back and says, "I didn't know what to do, you know? In 5th grade, he was suicidal. He was 10 and I just knew that I was really afraid for my child." There were other kids who were afraid as well—Ana Martinez, who was laughed at in math class; Colby Simpson, who was bullied every day at school; and Mark Browning, who was petrified that people would think he was crazy if they knew he was diagnosed with autism.

1

When I first met these eight students as part of my ethnography on academic identity development for youth with social and learning disabilities, it was not in a formal schooling context. Instead, I had the privilege of meeting them first in the activities they loved—debate team, music club, creative writing, and family time. I was immediately struck by the energy, passion, and leadership they displayed as they competed in national debate tournaments, performed in front of citywide audiences, and carried out their responsibilities at home.

It was not until I started observing them in their high school classrooms that I could truly appreciate how resilient they were. I had heard about their traumatic histories in elementary and middle school as well as their struggles with the special education system, but on paper they were all included in regular classrooms and the appropriate special support services were being provided. Each of them had individualized education plans (as required by law) that were carefully and intentionally implemented, supportive families who advocated on their behalf, well-meaning teachers, and high schools with strong inclusive education programs. What the paperwork could not account for were the implicit ways the students were positioned as academic failures. In the safety of their homes, the students would point directly to moments when peers would underestimate them, the smirks and snickers when they were called on, the loud "oooooo's" from the class when they gave a wrong answer, and how they noticed they were never chosen to lead. Once I was looking for them, I could see these practices everywhere. The pity or disappointment in teachers' voices when a student "didn't meet his potential," how they were blamed by school leadership when something went wrong, how both students and teachers would avoid calling on them to spare supposed humiliation, and countless other ways they were singled out as different. While this social positioning was often unintentional, these everyday interactions communicated low expectations, restricted opportunities, and revealed academic stereotypes, contributing to the damage to their sense of self. Perhaps even more than their labels, students were disabled by formal education.

DISABLED ACADEMIC IDENTITIES

At its core, this book is about the fear that the K–12 educational system instills in the minds of young people and what they do to survive the disabling educational practices they face. These practices, which often are taken for granted as a natural part of schooling, confront students with discouraging and stigmatizing messages about their intelligence, impacting their identities in the long term. In particular, it is the unconscious nature of these practices and the ways they are reproduced by teachers and students themselves that is most harmful to youth.

The eight case studies in this book explore how people learn and confirm assumptions about intellectual status in ways that pervade every human interaction. Each case illustrates how these interactions ripple out to drive future beliefs about the self and perceptions about others. Their in-depth accounts over 2 years show how adolescents, arguably in the most vulnerable and tumultuous time of their lives, attempt to make sense of their academic identities in the midst of disappointed comments about their "lack of potential." Their stories demonstrate the importance of accounting for individual histories and learning trajectories when making educational change, and the need to unlearn and change the disabling behaviors we practice every day.

Meet Anthony

While each chapter uses at least one case study to investigate these issues, the driving narrative of the book is that of 16-year-old Anthony Gustafson. Labeled with Asperger's syndrome at age 13, Anthony's ongoing reflections on what a disability might mean for his high school experience provide a useful frame for examining the complex role that formalized labels play in youth identity development. From the beginning, Anthony was never shy about talking about his new diagnosis, and we had regular conversations about how his latest label would impact his schooling, possible opportunities, and even the kind of person he thought he could be at school. Elements of his narrative are echoed in the other student accounts in each chapter, including pivotal negative school experiences in late elementary school, encounters with prejudice based on past behavior, the existence of clear personal goals that did not align with school-based learning, and struggles with the ever-shifting, contextual nature of being diagnosed with autism. More than anything, Anthony's story also offers the best representation of how forging relationships with students can help challenge deficit orientations about ability. Every interaction with Anthony pushed me to reconsider my own beliefs about potential, and the evolution of our collective experiences forced me to rethink my personal assumptions about how success is defined and what participation is valued. His narrative drives the central storyline of this book—that daily interactions and deep-seated cultural beliefs drive what young people do in their everyday lives and what they believe is possible.

I first met Anthony at the end of his first year of high school in the special education room, where I was attempting to recruit him to join a summer debate program I directed each year. His special education teacher invited me into the classroom, where I saw three students quietly working on collages, including Anthony, who was the tallest one in the room. During our interview, I was told he "liked attention and loved to make people laugh," hid behind "a wall of anger," "liked anything to do with the military," and "hated his disability." Considering that Anthony had been a part of four different research studies, attended eight different schools, and was thrown out of three different geometry classes, I could see why: He was accustomed to being told there was something "wrong" with him. During our first conversation that day, I could see how his goofy grin, jokes, and sarcastic comments could confirm these conclusions; however, I was impressed by his grasp of international politics and military history, and stunned by his ability to consider different perspectives. When I told him so, Anthony replied only with a shrug, "When they diagnosed me they said that autistic people have an obsession. I guess my thing is the military, since I'm supposed to have an obsession or whatever." He continued to describe himself as "the guy who gets thrown out of class," "the water boy," and "the retard," and talked about how he hated being called autistic because "then you're the guy everyone has to babysit." His confident exterior was disrupted when I asked him whether he wanted to join my debate camp. "Isn't debate for really smart kids? I don't think I'm good enough to be in debate. I'm big enough though, so maybe I'll intimidate everyone so they won't know what to say." Once again, his disability label became more than a set of services or a useful explanation for his learning problems. Instead, it challenged him to answer questions about who he was and, consequently, where he belonged.

Each of the three parts of this book begins with an "interlude," which continues the story of Anthony and his life in school, debate, and Young Marines, a police-shadowing program, as well as his family life. His experience exemplifies the power that formal schooling can have in restricting students' visions of themselves. From the beginning, Anthony revealed how being labeled with Asperger's syndrome often lowered his self-esteem about what he believed he was capable of doing and the kinds of activities where he would be welcome to participate. Even his strengths and background knowledge became part of his disability, and he had a difficult time escaping the assumptions that followed when he was categorized in this way. He was stuck in a self-fulfilling prophecy: He had to continue fulfilling people's expectations for abnormal behavior, not only because his participation was restricted by what people thought he could do, but because he was beginning to believe it himself. Anthony forces us to see firsthand how labels of ability can complicate identity development, in addition to the tensions students must resolve between how they view themselves and how they are viewed by others.

SOCIAL CONTEXT OF DISABILITY

In addition to Anthony, all of the other students in this book were especially vulnerable to these tensions because they were among the 4.2 million students with hidden, or "invisible," disabilities served under the Individuals with Disabilities Education Act (IDEA). These disabilities—defined as "both mental and physical conditions that are not immediately noticeable by an observer" (Matthews & Harrington, 2000)—include autism, learning disabilities, and reading and language impairments. For students labeled with non-obvious disabilities, the visibility factor can influence feelings of stigma or shame (Matthews & Harrington, 2000), which are compounded by the students' susceptibility to low self-esteem (Burden, 2008) and higher rates of absenteeism (Blackorby & Cameto, 2004). Similar to cases in this book, recent studies reveal that students vary in how and even whether they perceive themselves as disabled (Cory, 2005). Many feel pressured to "fix" their disability and are aware that knowledge of their disability alters the behaviors of others toward them (Kelly, 2005). As a result, youth actively manage the perceptions of others (Baines, 2012), often by attempting to "pass" or hide their disability (Edgerton, 1993; Olney & Brockelman, 2003). As with Tinsley and James, the negative elementary school experiences that students with invisible disabilities tend to have (Specht, Polgar, Willoughby, King, & Brown, 2000) further complicate their already tense histories with school as well as how they come to identify with their disability labels (Bagatell, 2007; Baines, 2011; Gallego, Durán, & Reyes, 2006).

Beyond students' immediate social and interpersonal experiences at school, there have been other means of framing the unproductive social dramas that touch their lives. Beginning with the work of Jules Henry (1963) 50 years ago, social scientists have long analyzed how students' experiences are driven and distorted by a system that organizes hierarchies based on social differences. Categories (such as Attention Deficit Disorder and Specific Learning Disability) emerge out of competitive intellectual status systems designed for some students to succeed while others fail. Unclear biological evidence for diagnoses such as autism have led many researchers and activists in disability studies to find the concept of autism problematic (Jack, 2011; Timimi, 2011). This move to investigate the social construction of disability challenges the use of medical rhetoric as a way of categorizing individuals and distracting from issues within social systems (Molloy & Vasil, 2002). In light of this framework, studies of students' negative experiences in school become more than a collection of personal complaints and part of a more pervasive tradition of blaming individual students for system failure. At the same time, while the "social construction of disability" idea is well established in disability studies literature (e.g., Cousin, Diaz, Flores, & Hernandez, 1995; Dudley-Marling, 2004; Mehan, 1996; Varenne & McDermott, 1998), how these processes work in the lives of high school students remains largely abstract. Conversations about the more sinister forces at play when a student is called "lazy" or "unmotivated" persist at academic conferences, but rarely reach the teachers and families who are trying desperately to transform a child into someone the school can be proud of. And so the process of disablement continues, and "at-risk" or "disabled" students are left wondering what they did wrong.

Positioned Participation and Identity Development

Efforts to explain the sociocultural dynamics at work in these cases unfortunately include many concepts that are often difficult to define and see in the world, making it challenging to come to a consensus about their meaning. "Identity" is one of these terms, along with "participation." In this book, I conceptualize *identity* as Dorothy Holland and colleagues do, as self-understandings and imaginings produced through sociocultural relations, developed and lived through everyday activity. Consequently, "identities are a key means through which people care about and care for what is going on around them" (Holland, Lachicotte, Skinner, & Cain, 1998, p. 5). Given the often-contentious role of schooling in the lives of youth who have been labeled "learning disabled," I look at "academic identities," which I define as personal perceptions of academic ability resulting from an ongoing process of self-understanding in relation to others, the demands of educational contexts, cultural definitions of academic success, and personal interests.

Defining academic identities in this way helps consider how students perceive themselves as learners and relate to the goals and expectations of formal education. The experiences and relationships students go through as a result of their difficulties in school create unique tensions that they must resolve. In addition to the typical turbulence of adolescence, they must resolve conflicts that arise when school says they are not "smart" when they believe that they are. They have to weigh what school values as important and what they enjoy doing. Over the course of their experiences in school, they have to figure out what choices they will make and what pathways they will pursue, and whether this will be aligned with expectations of others.

To help clarify how this takes place, it is also important to conceptualize "participation." Rather than the colloquial understanding of participation as momentary involvement or attendance, this book considers the lifetime trajectories of social practice across diverse contexts. As framed by Ole Dreier (2009), this view of participation deals with the question of what people are a part of and in what manner they participate in diverse contexts as they occupy different positions with varying scopes of possibility. In Chapter 2, I discuss viewing "ability as agency," which is an extension of Amartya Sen's capabilities framework in combination with Rom Harré's positioning theory. It connects to the capabilities framework in that it considers the relationship between people's capability and freedom to choose among various sets of opportunities. The ability as agency idea conceptualizes "ability development" as driven by people's desire to acquire the capabilities they need to drive the direction of their own lives and exercise agency. Such capabilities change and develop as people continue to interact and participate with others. Where positioning theory comes in, is in describing how interactions with others are constantly driven by social patterns in power relationships that affect a person's capacity to act or access certain valued opportunities. The nature of the contexts themselves shape how positioning takes place, as well as how people gain meaning from their participation and whether they are able to pursue their personal concerns.

The difficult part, though, is that there are often conflicting norms and values in different contexts, and therefore "persons face the challenge of composing each complex life across diverse contexts . . . to avoid contradictions between its parts getting in the way of preserving what matters most to them" (Dreier, 2009, p. 196). While formal learning in school may be a positive experience for many students, others can experience a disconnect between their actions and goals and what the school views as valued participation. Students with diagnosed disabilities are vulnerable by definition, as they somehow "lack" what it takes to achieve "success" as defined by formal schooling. Weinstein (2002) elaborates on the importance of interrupting the self-fulfilling prophecy in education.

> Paying attention simply to perceptions or to teachers alone leads to an exceedingly narrow perspective on the phenomenon . . . In broadening our explanation, we need to understand that those who judge children's performance and capability are embedded in complex and changing organizational, cultural, and historic contexts that extend beyond the teacher–student relationship. (p. 67)

"Too Much Failure": Histories of Struggle over Time

Anthony's case demonstrates how long histories of negative positioning make it increasingly more difficult for targeted support efforts to make any lasting improvement. Structured learning environments in 1st and 2nd grades, along with opportunities to display his early skill in public speaking, initially helped alleviate some of his problems with temper tantrums, interrupting teachers, and working in groups. Over time, however, his contributions in class became less desirable to his teachers. In 4th grade, his mother, Greta, remembers, "I would pick him up on Mondays because that was my day off, and you could hear her say, 'Does anyone else besides Anthony know the answer?' So even though he was participating a lot early on, he learned not to say anything." The roller coaster continued with Greta's desperate attempts to figure out what was wrong, pulling him out of different schools and taking him to doctors and a children's health organization that diagnosed him with severe depression, executive functioning disorder, and a nonverbal learning disability. In the course of a year, the kid who never wanted to miss school wanted to miss it all the time, and he was told he was "lazy and not working up to his potential." After years of switching schools, home schooling, tutoring, and medication, Anthony and his family finally found a successful learning environment in a private Christian school. The success was short-lived, though, ironically because he lacked the organizational and social skills from consistency, familiarity, and an established social circle. As his mother describes,

> Basically, here was this kid, who had been through all this, he was defiant, doing this kind of stupid behavior, and [his teacher] would say, "We can't do anything if he doesn't want to do it," and I mean yeah, I don't know what to do either, you know? I'm relying on the professionals. They just say, "Put him on medication," but no, he has to be adequately assessed! We've just been through the ringer. I'm sorry, it's just been painful, it's like a roller coaster, and we keep thinking it is never gonna end. And now when he burns bridges with kids or teachers he's like, "I need to go to another school." And we're not going to another school anymore, you know? There are schools for autism or Aspie kids but he doesn't want to be associated with those kids. But how do we turn it around?

Over the course of this battle with schooling, Anthony continued to find private outlets for his interests, in an attempt to "preserve what matters most" (Dreier, 2009, p. 196). From young military programs to political history books, he somehow managed to find ways to "compose life in diverse contexts" and compartmentalize his passions from his negative academic history. Anthony is not alone in these efforts. Throughout this book, different students strive to reposition themselves, or at least find a place where they can succeed. As Greta points out, "Kids need to fail, but too much failure for a child like Anthony is not a good thing either."

CROSS-CONTEXT ETHNOGRAPHY

To better understand the role of identity processes in learning and position-ing dynamics across contexts and over time, we (a team of four education re-searchers) set out to observe what a lack of time and resources often prevents educators from seeing: the everyday lives of youth in diverse contexts. As part of a 2-year team ethnography supported by the Learning in Informal and For-mal Environments (LIFE) Center at the University of Washington, we were able to witness the variety of ways young people experienced and dealt with disabling academic histories like Anthony's. There were nine young people (from three different public high schools in California and Washington State) who were selected based on their involvement in extracurricular pursuits, in-cluding a debate team, a music program, and an ecology program. Since we believed that people live their lives by participating in many materially and so-cially arranged contexts, we studied the same youth in everyday contexts such as formal schooling, home contexts, and community settings. In addition to what resulted in 2,000 hours of audio- and video-recorded observations and supplemental fieldnotes, we performed monthly interviews with each of the students, their peers, families, teachers, and instructors. These interviews not only provided valuable member checks to ensure the accuracy of our analyses, but also offered in-depth reflections on how students and the primary people in their lives viewed their behavior.

"You Don't Belong Here": Labels and Youth Reactions

Over the course of those 2 years, we documented shifts in how students identified with academic learning and perceived their abilities as a result of these experiences. Although I expected to see evidence of inequitable school-ing structures, given the tracking that often occurs in public schools, I was surprised by the extent of students' awareness of how they were being posi-tioned in terms of intellectual status. In contrast to the dynamic and engag-ing learning experiences they had outside school, they described school as a place where they were always "stuck," where according to James Ovill, "they label you, and it's over." Another student, Spencer MacArthur, adds, "I hated being called ADD. Because it's like, 'hey he has that.' I don't want something people just put on me. People look at you and think you're 'that,' they label you." For Anthony, perceptions about his potential and behavior threatened his involvement in debate, an activity typically associated with advanced placement students. Despite a successful experience in my sum-mer debate program, he was thrown out of debate during the year after a disagreement with the new coach, Rebecca Miller. After he was whispering and laughing with his neighbor during a lecture, she singled him out saying, "Anthony, that isn't your assigned seat. You don't even have an assigned seat. What are you even doing here? I asked you to leave before. You don't belong here."

While their participation was clearly situated within institutional structures of academic achievement and dependent on interactions with others, the students were not powerless; they regularly exercised their agency by pushing back against socially accepted structures of power and success. In the words of Devin Foster, they "had to prove that everyone is wrong." Colby Simpson elaborates, "People are going to underestimate you no matter what, you have to show them . . . you have to put a bit of your soul on the line." Despite being kicked out of debate, Anthony spent every day standing outside the debate room, greeting his teammates and looking in at what they were doing. As soon as the coach left the team, he rejoined, saying, "Might as well . . . I guess I can do this." Witnessing and listening to how their positions shifted with each setting, activity, and community, showed how youth deliberately asserted powerful personal stances to resolve the mismatch between how they viewed themselves and how they were viewed by others. Their stories painted a picture of their battle to be valued by others despite their histories in school. Appreciating and understanding these complex, sophisticated, and dynamic self-positioning moves reminds us that these students' plight stems from relational sources—in the words of Professor Ray McDermott, "One cannot be learning disabled alone."

ORGANIZATION OF BOOK

The conceptual arc of this book is divided into three parts, which show how and why disabling practices must be recognized, understood, and disrupted to support student learning and strong identities. To make this case, the first two parts show how youth become "disabled" by social interactions and negative assumptions about their abilities, how these experiences impact their capacity to control the direction of their lives, and how they push back against such constraints. They present an explanation of the social processes of disablement, how young people preserve what is important to them, and the ways in which positioning can expand or restrict participation and the development of academic identities. The final part discusses how understanding educational positioning can facilitate the process of "unlearning disability." It reviews examples from alternative education and informal learning to better understand specific efforts to disrupt disablement, including flexible school structures, ability-oriented mindsets for teaching, and youth-driven cultural transformation.

In the first chapter, I begin with a discussion of social factors that drive subjective perceptions of ability and academic failure. Continuing with the case of Anthony Gustafson, I consider the role of bias and other social influences on decisionmaking in special education, along with the impact on students' lives and identities. Anthony's case helps illustrate how students struggle to take ownership in the midst of disabling forces, and introduces some of the more hidden impacts of disabling practices. The second chapter in Part I more specifically frames how young people resolve tensions between their own perceptions of their abilities and how others view them. It explains a framework for examining student motives behind developing abilities and how students work to expand their "scopes of possibilities." To illustrate how these processes take place, it focuses on Tinsley Hawkins, a 10th-grader diagnosed with a speech/learning processing disorder. This case describes Tinsley's early experiences dealing with pressure in school and examines how these processes of disablement take place for her. Like Anthony, her experience shows how she was not helpless in the midst of this positioning. As the writer of three 140-page novels, she privately contradicted perceptions that limited her to the category "language impaired." This case demonstrates how students reflect on this process, how they can position themselves as capable despite the perceptions of others, and how they pursue their own deep learning practices outside school.

The two chapters in Part II rely on four student cases to examine the various impacts of disabling practices and how young people continue to resist them. Chapter 3 explores the influence of academic stereotypes on youth opportunities and how young people continue to develop abilities in places they are told they do not belong. In the case of Spencer MacArthur, a 10th-grader who was diagnosed with attention deficit disorder in the midst of a drawn-out court process, assumptions about his past behavior resulted in lower expectations for his future and limited beliefs about his potential. In addition to how students live under the oppressive shadow of personal histories, they also face racial and gender stereotypes about who can participate. Devin Foster demonstrates how he maintained persistent involvement in speech and debate, challenging perceptions that "students like him" did not belong in such a rigorous academic activity. This chapter considers the intersection of race and disability as well as how high school students often can echo disabling discourse based on societal stereotypes. Devin's case shows how social inequities and stereotypes can threaten students' trajectories of participation. In addition to exemplifying how these practices can play out over a longer period of time, Chapter 3 also examines the positive personal and academic supports that enabled Devin to gain respect and acceptance in an "intellectual" activity. In Chapter 4, two cases illustrate how young people relate to disability labels and how their identification can impact their choices, actions, and participation. The chapter discusses how youth continue to resist disabling practices to achieve their goals and respond to disablement in a variety of ways. The case of Mark Browning, who views himself as a "recovering autistic," reveals the potential threat that being labeled with autism could pose to his goal of being viewed as "smart" in school. Instead of wanting to fit school-based expectations, James Ovill demonstrates how students can be motivated to distance themselves from the school setting in order to pursue their desired future—in his case, becoming a "scientist," rather than only being seen as "ADD." Both cases consider the influence of students' outside lives in the development of their academic identities. Their stories show how students face academic identity crises as they come to terms with their disability label, deal with conflicting school and family expectations, and discover what they desire for their own futures. This chapter builds on earlier chapters by framing how social processes of disablement impact adolescent identities that are always fragile and in motion over the course of their lives.

The final part contains three chapters that consider ways to disrupt disablement and "unlearn" disabling practices. Chapter 5 uses the case of an alternative school to look at school-based efforts to encourage youth pride and considers how flexible, individualized structures can help promote the possibility of pride in disability. The chapter takes a closer look at the experiences of one student, Colby Simpson, to explore ideas for cultural change and how essential such change is for the emotional health of all students. Chapter 6 argues for a shift in mindset regarding youth success and discusses potential supports that can help drive a practical theory of change. It offers three examples of teacher tools that can promote more flexible, supportive ideas about intelligence, and uses them to emphasize the importance of building in opportunities for active youth participation. The final chapter considers the relational challenges of developing a culture that privileges the power of youth. It uses the story of Ana Martinez and her experiences on the Hillside debate team to explore ways to build transformative group cultures. It concludes with an argument for the importance of fostering youth-driven cultures, where young people play an active role in confronting rigid notions of success, and adult–student relationships help challenge disabling practices.

From Pitying the Victim to Self-Critique

The cases in this book demonstrate how important mentorship, support, and strong relationships can be in helping students figure out what they care about, make key choices, navigate obstacles, and pursue future pathways. While they are aware of the hardships that accompany learning disabilities, and recognize the necessary support that individualized interventions provide, the students question what makes disability labels relevant in the first place and what that implies about their learning. The young people in the chapters that follow resent the assumptions people make about their potential and how quickly a single moment can define and solidify expectations about how they will act in the future and what they can do. They complain that people simplify their troubles, and feel threatened by changes that fail to recognize who they are. More than anything, they dread the pity and sympathy that the word *special* entails.

The social dynamics at play in this positioning—and the emotional turmoil that follows—are very real, but often subtle. It is impossible to point to one culprit and quickly remedy the problem. In an interview with Devin Foster's mother, she points out, "Schools categorize kids into good students and bad students. Or who has potential. But I'm not going to even put it as a school or school district problem. It's a community problem." Without exploring the tensions between how students pursue their concerns and the role we all play in preventing them from doing so, it will be difficult to ever truly revise educational paradigms. Unfortunately, when tensions are complex, they often become abstract and change becomes difficult. It is much easier to focus our efforts on addressing what the student failed to accomplish and later imagine that we have done everything we can do.

Instead, stories like Anthony's remind us to think more broadly about how every interaction influences how young people view their potential. As author Toni Morrison (2007) puts it, people must move away from "the comfort of pitying" victims to "interrogating themselves for the smashing" (p. xii). While individualized supports are an important first step to improving student learning, it is vital that the more invisible and entrenched disabling practices are not simply recognized, but unlearned. Revising this reality will be essential as long as the purpose of education continues to be to expand, not restrict, students' visions of themselves, what they can do, and what they believe is possible. Only then will "inclusive education" become something that is more than just implemented, but lived.

Part I

POSITIONING AND THE PRODUCTION OF DISABLED IDENTITIES

There's one quote I love by e.e. cummings: "To be nobody-but-yourself—in a world which is doing its best, night and day, to make you everybody else—means to fight the hardest battle which any human being can fight; and never stop fighting." I believe that. First, you have to stop being somebody else, then you have to define yourself, then you have to start being that person.

—Tinsley Hawkins, 15

The Water Boy

In high school, summers are a pause, an interlude before the dramas of friendship and the pressures of pleasing people begin once again. Three weeks before vacation is torture for students, and as I enter Hillside High for the first time, the walls of the building reverberate with anticipation for the months to come. My heels click down the hallway, echoing the sound of classroom clocks, watched by student eyes, ticking down the seconds to summer.

All of the classroom doors look the same, but eventually I reach the one at the end of the hallway. Ms. Hayes, one of the special education teachers, is expecting me, and her warm, ecstatic greeting makes me feel better about intruding into her life and the lives of her students. As we sit down for our meeting, I see three students in the classroom, quietly working. "We won't bother them," she whispered, noticing my gaze. "We'll just keep our voices down."

It seems wrong to talk about people while they are in the room, but the students behind us do not seem to mind. Quietly, they cut pictures out of magazines and paste them onto construction paper with the words "Coat of Arms" scrawled across the top. As Ms. Hayes speaks, I can't help but peek back at the students to spy on what they are doing. One of the boys looks up from his paper, smiles sarcastically, and gives me an exaggerated thumbs-up. He is taller than the others, with close-cropped blond hair and glasses with small frames. Except for the paper in front of him and the glue stick in his hand, it would be easy to mistake him for a teacher. "Who is he?" I ask Ms. Hayes. "Oh, that's just Anthony Gustafson."

I had heard about Anthony from his instructional aide, who had suggested I recruit him to be part of the summer debate program I recently had started along with the study I had embarked on. As I speak to Ms. Hayes, he occasionally looks over and smiles with a grin that is at once mischievous, tired, and bored. To his surprise, I pick up my notebook and recorder and take a seat next to him. He says hello in a measured, polite voice at first without looking at me. Before I can respond, he quickly swivels to face me and speaks in an exaggerated cadence, making his voice go up and down with every word, all with a goofy grin on his face: "How are you doing this lovely day?" I smile, giving the obligatory, "Fine, how are you?" to which he responds, "Fantastic! Thanks for asking!" I explain that I love debate and that I want to discuss a few issues with him to see what he thinks. Understandably, he looks puzzled by my vague explanation but seems game for whatever challenge I can throw at him, especially if it will get him out of pasting magazine pictures onto a piece of paper.

"What do you think about nuclear weapons?" I smile at his stunned expression, figuring that surprise would be the best way to connect with him, since he acted as if he had seen it all. I continued, "When I was on the debate team, I had to argue about whether the possession of nuclear weapons was immoral. What do you think about the issue?" He gathered his thoughts before seriously answering, "That's a controversial issue. It depends on which country you are talking about and what their reasons are for having nuclear weapons. During the Cold War, some think the threat of mutually assured destruction was the only way to go, although we came pretty close during the Cuban missile crisis. . . ." As he continued to list off different sides of the argument, he did so with the ease of a polished politician. Inside, I was stunned, but I kept my face carefully blank. With all of his jumping back and forth between different perspectives, I couldn't help but wonder how he could ever be labeled autistic. As if reading my mind, Anthony interrupted himself, "If you're wondering how I know all this stuff, it's just 'cause of my Asperger's. When they diagnosed me at 13 they said autistic people have an obsession with one thing. I guess my thing is anything having to do with the military, since I'm supposed to have an obsession. And I know a lot about it too, since my dad was in Special Forces. What do you want to talk about next?"

We spoke for the entire 90 minutes, and when it was over, I couldn't wait to have him at my debate camp. "Isn't debate for really smart kids? I don't think I'm good enough to be in debate. I'm big enough though, so maybe I'll intimidate everyone so they won't know what to say. You know my dad calls me man-boy?" "You definitely are good enough! All we are going to do is discuss and argue issues like the ones we just talked about." "I'll think about it. I have to talk to my mom." "I hope you decide to join; we'd be lucky to have you."

Anthony did join debate that summer and was, in fact, early on the first day. As I struggled up the stairs with my supplies, he swiftly whisked the boxes out of my hands, loading them into the room with ease. He suddenly launched into a story about a police raid he had witnessed the night before. It was a tale worthy of a major cable network channel, complete with guns, men in uniform, drugs, and rolls of caution tape. Anthony was in the police car in the midst of the action, wearing a bulletproof jacket, watching it all. The story was unbelievable, and as I rushed around the room finishing preparations, I was only half-listening. He sounded so into it, but I doubted the truth of his story, as I also did during our first meeting after hearing about his dad's "top-secret missions" with the U.S. Coast Guard's Special Forces. I had no reason not to believe him, but I had taught too many students who preferred the imaginary over real life and I had gotten cynical. We would wait and see.

"Do you know anyone in the debate class, Anthony?" I asked. "I don't really hang out with those kids, but I'm sure I know who some of them are." He turned to face me, a desk in his hands and a glint in his eye. "As long as there are a few hot girls, I'll be fine." It was 7:45, and students were beginning to file into the room, looking uncomfortable and silent. Everyone looked so young compared with 16-year-old Anthony, who sat lounging in a chair on the opposite side of the room, like a nonchalant businessman in his corner office. "Hi, I'm Anthony, how are you guys doing? Looking forward to debating with you." The others mumbled unintelligible responses and kept their eyes to the ground.

After a few team-building exercises, the atmosphere in the room had lightened considerably and they were ready for their first structured debate. The debate was modeled after the U.S. Congress, and students were required to come up with three points to support their stance on same-sex schools. As soon as I asked for the first volunteer, Anthony's hand shot up before anyone else's. While they were allowed to bring up their notes, Anthony left his paper behind, confidently striding up to the front of the room, even though I had given them the option of staying seated in their place. In a loud, deep voice, he began, "Today, I will discuss having same-sex schools. My first point is, look at the pregnancy rates, they're skyrocketing." Enjoying the silence in the room, he raised both hands, nodding and whispering, "skyrocketing." A few students smirked at one another and there was a smattering of muffled giggles. "And um, you know, there's just the distraction, and you just don't need that, you need to learn . . . you need to learn." Anthony's eyes darted to the clock and then back at the audience. "Um, my second point, what is my second point, um . . . " He looked at me with a slightly desperate expression. "Can you give us more time to prepare these things? God!" The laughter that followed was much louder and more confident than before as everyone waited for what he would say next. Snapping his fingers, Anthony looked at his audience and grinned, "What was my second point? I forgot it, no I had the whole speech, um, I can't think of anything. I had it too, and then it just, went away. Like magic. How much more time?" Seeing the time left on the clock, he made an exaggerated, shocked facial expression, getting more laughter from the class as one student started humming the theme from "Jeopardy." "So how's everybody doing today?" One girl prompted him to say he was "open for cross-examination," which was how I had instructed them to end their speeches. "Okay, I'm open for cross-examination." The class laughed as a few students stood up to ask him questions. When it was time for him to sit down, he hung his head and walked with exaggerated, sheepish steps back to his seat, leading to even more laughter from the other debaters.

Over the weeks, the laughter got louder and students became more confident in their comments in reaction to his speeches. It was strange because Anthony's speeches were becoming clearer, more detailed, with more support and evidence than many of the others. He was starting to be able to remember his first two points, but still struggled with his conclusions. After that first day, I reminded students to support one another, cracked down on the laughter, and asked students to applaud for each speaker. My rules didn't matter much, though, because it was almost as if Anthony could hear the laughter in their silence. Regardless of how complete and eloquent his first two points were, he would revert to a joke, the plot from a popular movie, or a goofy example as his third point, which was greeted with giggles or groans from the class. At the end of the 4 weeks, the students dressed up in suits for a mock debate tournament during the day, culminating in a performance for the parents in the evening. Anthony was excited about dressing up in his suit, boasting to the others about how good he looked in slacks and how he would have to get up early to polish his dress shoes. The topic was "A parliamentary form of government is preferable to the U.S. presidential system." Each student would debate another student in separate rooms, and parents could choose whom to watch.

As usual, Anthony arrived early, this time with his mother Greta and his father Anthony, Sr., an imposing man who introduced himself with a frighteningly firm handshake. In addition to his notepad, Anthony was carrying a bouquet of flowers, which he handed to me as we posed for a picture. Although they had not been assigned the task of setting up, Greta quickly laid out fancy napkins and two silver coffee urns, with plates of homemade cookies for the parents. Anthony, Sr., started lifting tables, handing chairs to Anthony to arrange in the main room. There was not a single goofy grin on Anthony's face as he said, "Yes, sir" and did as he was told.

When it was time to debate, Anthony had one of the biggest audiences, which worried me at first because I did not know what to expect. His first few speeches went smoothly, and both students respectfully asked each other questions during cross-examination. Before his final speech, Anthony paused for a moment, smiling at the audience as I held my breath.

> My opponent says that stability and justice is more important than the people's rights. But you can't have stability or justice without the people's rights. I would rather live free or die . . . like the New Hampshire license plate. My opponent also says that third parties take away from votes from the two main parties, but third parties represent more people, and it protects their rights because you aren't lumped into two main par-

ties. He also said the President is elected more directly, but a 33.3% vote is what's needed to get the President in office, Parliament is the majority of . . . PMs . . . no, MPs, my bad. And with a majority of those it's more fair to the leader I guess, and umm . . . (pause). Obviously, I'm at a loss for words right now, I think you should take that into consideration and vote him as the winner, I just can't think.

I was pleased with his arguments and how he remained entirely focused in front of dozens of people, including his parents. I was disappointed when Anthony and everyone else talked only about how he fell apart in the last few seconds, forgetting what had come before. I didn't know how Anthony felt that night, but he was an energetic participant in the end-of-program BBQ the next day. Everyone became nostalgic about the end of camp, and Anthony shook hands and hugged the others, saying what a good job they did. He seemed like part of the team, and one of the girls said, "It really wouldn't have been the same without him." Another boy responded, "And definitely not as fun without his speeches!"

When I next saw Anthony, it was a few weeks into the school year at the end of debate class. I had heard he was having difficulty with the new debate coach as well as the transition from summer camp culture to a more formal debate class. As I watched, Anthony slumped in his chair and looked down at the desk. He leaned over to whisper to the boy next to him, and they both unsuccessfully attempted to stifle their laughter. None of the other students seemed surprised by their snickers, but unlike the summer when they would engage with his jokes, they deliberately averted their eyes and stared up intently at the coach. It was clear this was not unusual behavior, and I knew he had been asked to leave the class before. When I asked him about this, Anthony shrugged and said, "I'm always getting thrown out of class. I'm just the guy that teachers throw out of class." During this class, though, Anthony had arrived with a notebook. After his initial whispers to his neighbor, he began taking notes on the lecture. The coach had already had enough. "Anthony, that isn't your assigned seat. You don't even have an assigned seat. What are you even doing here? I asked you to leave before. You don't belong here." "My BS meter has had enough," Anthony muttered as he gathered his stuff and left the room.

After that day, Anthony continued to stand at the doorway of the debate class to say hello to his friends before returning to the special education tutorial class. "I'm the debate water boy. I'm the football water boy, so I thought the debate team needed one too!" While his debate career seemed over before it even began, he shrugged it off, continuing to tell me stories about police raids and military missions, stories that were still a mystery to me.

Chapter 1

Social Processes of Disablement

The "water boy" is a common character in U.S. secondary education. Beyond dealing with academics and pressures to succeed, adolescents regularly engage in a battle to be able to pursue their own passions, interests, and goals, no matter how much they shift and change. In short, young people work hard to be seen as worthy enough to play the game. It is difficult for them to forget any moment that communicates a more sinister message—that they will, for some reason, be unable to accomplish the skills necessary to achieve their goals or that they have failed to belong to the more valued, prized group of performers. In an age when academic learning has become the socially accepted definition and gateway to success, being labeled as learning deficient can threaten the possibility that their imagined identities can ever become reality. They are designated to watch from the sidelines, destined to cater to the needs of others. While they are officially included in the group, they are, in effect, socially excluded.

Regardless of disability status, schools have long played a central role in sorting children according to abilities that matter most to socially accepted notions of "success" (McDermott, 1993; Olson, 2009; Pope, 2001). The issue is that beliefs about intelligence and assumptions about valued abilities are often narrowly defined, despite the past 30 years of research into the diverse processes of human learning (Dweck, 2006; Gardner, 1983; Rose, Meyer, & Hitchcock, 2005). Kirsten Olson (2009) argues that such outdated ideas about knowledge and human potential result in "wounds of underestimation," which "instruct us in our own inferiority" (Illich, 1971, p. 29) and teach us to underestimate ourselves. While implicit school values such as the ability to work rapidly and accurately are only a small part of what is required in the world, they pervade everyday actions and shape assumptions about who can succeed, thus impacting the nature of student learning experiences. Students as young as 1st-graders are aware of this differential treatment and learn clues (such as how much help they receive from teachers) to developing ideas about smartness and where they fit within the classroom achievement hierarchy (Weinstein, 2002). The model of the academic pecking order—where only a select few can succeed—so often is assumed to be an inherent aspect of schooling itself that it is difficult to see the problems with it (Pope,

2001). As Beth Ferri and David Connor (2007) point out, "In other words, because the status quo works well for the dominant group, students from non-dominant groups experience the imbalance of power and are required to either fit into the existing structures or to risk being relegated to alternative or 'special' classrooms or schools" (p. 130).

ACADEMIC FAILURE: WHO IS TO BLAME?

It is crucial not only to examine how success is defined and perceived, but also to consider who is viewed as responsible for that success or, conversely, for that failure. Current approaches to assessment and instruction have a tendency to frame educational success as solely a matter of individual effort and to claim that those who do not succeed simply did not try hard enough (Mehan, 2008). Shifting the blame for underperformance or disengagement solely to the child largely ignores the situated and complex nature of learning established over the past 2 decades (Lave, 1987; Lave & Wenger, 1991; Pea & Brown, 1991). The danger of doing so is that "this mode of legitimating stratification blames individuals for their failure to attain a higher status and deflects attention from the system itself" (Mehan, 2008, p. 46). In essence, such a mindset puts some of the most powerless students under constant public scrutiny, without the tools to improve their status or image. The focus of conversations about educational improvement becomes more about what single individuals are doing wrong, and less about how the system itself is constructed to perpetuate cycles of failure from its most vulnerable students.

Instead, sociocultural models of disability frame educational success or failure as a product of how our culture is organized (Collins, 2013; Mc-Dermott, Goldman, & Varenne, 2006). This idea implies that students' actions and decisions stem not only from their own desires or interactions with others but also from larger cultural perceptions about ability. In short, as Kathleen Collins (2013) affirms, "The mediational means and habits of mind of the learning community, the opportunities they afford, the constraints they impose, and the transformations that they undergo, must all be considered" (p. 4). The idea that individual participation with others can transform their learning experience is consistent with Vygotsky's concept of the mind. In his studies of children with severe disabilities, he expresses the belief that children are full of unrealized potential and, when afforded creative resources, are able to build upon their natural strengths. Moreover, he maintains that through continued interactions with their sociocultural world, children can develop higher mental functions through "overcompensating" for biological "impediments." However, "in order that the child mediate, make sense of, and interact in a meaningful way with the environment, he or she must have access to and acquire a multitude of psychological tools . . . to shape and organize the world" (Knox & Stevens, 1993, p. 15). Depending on the nature of the supports and opportunities available for students to discover and display their strengths, it is possible for disabilities to be more relevant in some contexts as opposed to others. In Anthony's case, it came as little surprise to his math teachers that he was labeled with a social disability, especially when it came to working with others; on the other hand, in his after-school police shadowing program, he was a clear choice for the leadership award. Similarly, Collins's case study of Jay revealed that varying supports and tools helped him exhibit different abilities as well as disabilities, depending on the activity.

This idea that the same person can display drastically different levels of competence in different settings, depending on the contextual arrangements and whether he or she is pushed to perform or expected to fail, is not new. In the 1970s, for instance, Rosalind Oppenheim (1974) found that failure to perform can often be linked to a lack of engagement as opposed to an inability to comprehend the material. Unfortunately, perceived deficiencies continue to be discussed as static, internal traits unlikely to be permanently improved. Even notably successful individuals are dismissed as exceptions to the rule, "statistical outliers," or even accused of being misdiagnosed, particularly with disabilities such as autism (Biklen, 2005). When I share stories of Anthony's success on his high school debate team, most people react by questioning whether he actually should have been labeled with Asperger's syndrome or knowingly conclude, "Well, if he did well in debate, he must have just been high-functioning." It follows that such logic would make it impossible to ever be simultaneously successful and disabled, discouraging students from identifying proudly with something perceived as so antithetical to success.

Subjective Perceptions of Ability

The question of responsibility for academic failure is not only a matter of conceptual framing, but a phenomenon that regularly manifests itself in the lives of adolescents in disturbing and life-altering ways. Perceptions of ability are deeply driven by a host of influencing factors—as McDermott (1993) reminds us, everyone is a part of the choreography that produces moments for degradation or praise. According to Harry and Klingner(2006), three disability categories under IDEA are most easily seen as social constructions based on subjective ideas about normalcy: educable mental retardation (EMR), emotional/behavioral disorder (EBD), and specific learning disability (SLD or LD), along with attention deficit hyperactivity disorder, which is not recognized by IDEA. Harry and colleagues continue, "Although we view these features as pathological, the interpretation is essentially based on societal norms for development and learning, not on measurable facts" (p. 3). The impact of these individual judgments continues to affect an increasing number of students, as the rates of LD identification have increased almost sixfold in the past 40 years (National Research Council, 2002).

Subjective decisions impact students in a multitude of ways. Personal perceptions about learning and behavior permeate the entire evaluation process, from even the slightest suspicion of "discrepancy." Despite seemingly objective evaluative measures, decisions about testing (whom to test, what test to use, how to interpret responses, and how to weight results) can alter outcomes about special education placement. Such decisions can be driven by stereotypes, bias, and powerful predispositions to blame particular populations of children, however unconscious these judgments might be. Often based in unofficial beliefs about race-linked factors, gender and ethnicity biases, and assumptions about socioeconomic status, negative mindsets can significantly impact how students are identified, placed, and served, especially for African American children (Losen & Orfield, 2005). While the children themselves can be the subject of implicit blame for learning difficulties, so are their families, who are frequently the scapegoat in the minds of school personnel (Harry, Klingner, Sturges, & Moore, 2005). Consequently, less attention is paid to other factors, such as the influence of a disorderly classroom atmosphere on student behavior, changes in the IQ score cutoff point, or pressures for psychologists to identify children for special education (Harry et al., 2005; Kellam, Ling, Merisca, Brown, & Ialongo, 1998; Losen & Orfield, 2005).

Racial bias also can result in the needless isolation of minority students with disabilities from their nondisabled peers, and the effects of this isolation are further augmented by inadequate special education services in high-poverty urban schools (Losen & Orfield, 2005). These negative impacts are particularly intensified when disability intersects with factors such as gender and ethnicity and the stereotypes that accompany them (Wehmeyer, 2008). Moreover, schools and teachers lacking sufficient supports for inclusive education have been known to address disciplinary problems or a lack of resources by referring students to special education (National Research Council, 2002). As Harry, Kligner, and Cramer (2007) support:

> Because of the law's requirement for signs of intrinsic deficit as criteria for services, school personnel often engage in a search for such a deficit without taking into account the numerous contradictions and discrepancies in the construct of disability . . . The focus on intrinsic deficit tends to trump issues of context, resulting in a search that excludes serious consideration of the many risks inherent in schooling itself. (p. 17)

Social influences on decisionmaking can not only increase the likelihood for special education placement, but also seriously impact how students perceive themselves as learners (Harry & Klingner, 2006; Keefe, Moore, & Duff, 2006). Not only do students begin to internalize negative beliefs about their potential, but, as with Anthony, but they also perceive the classroom as a place where they have little control. According to Wehmeyer (2008), students with disabilities are particularly susceptible to restricted decision-making opportunities, which can interfere with the development of self-determination, identity, and an adolescent's move toward autonomy. In this way, the seemingly innocent "science" of sorting students to better identify their learning needs can result in unintended social stratification. Regardless of how objective these measures might seem, their implementation and impact are deeply social and subject to human interference, with significant ramifications for children. As Harry and colleagues (2005) elaborate, "We do not always know if measured performance reflects ability . . . If the process is a matter of social decision-making that leads to questionable outcomes, then there is clearly a problem" (p. 72).

The role of subjectivity in the labeling process is a "chicken and egg" problem, with questions of whether a student's behavior drives people's perceptions of ability or whether assumptions about normalcy instead impact a student's experience and subsequent actions. Anthony, for instance, enjoyed his early years in school and was praised for his early talent in public speaking. As he continued in school, the descriptor "strong speaker" became "disruptive interruption," as driven by the perceptions of those around him. Occasional problems working with others soon became defiance and a lack of motivation in class, along with struggles with organization. Visits with psychologists and participation in three different research studies produced multiple explanations for what was "wrong" with Anthony. Diagnoses ranged from severe depression to executive functioning disorder, and then moved to a nonverbal learning disability. Initial studies concluded he did not have autism, whereas a year later he had Asperger's syndrome. Early attempts to get an individualized education plan (IEP) were denied, but later in high school he was provided with necessary supports only because he was "lucky" enough to get a qualified disability label. In this way, the impetus to improve the social conditions that were already driving the manifestation of his "disability" could only come from finding something wrong with Anthony, the individual. As with the change in his participation from debate camp to the debate class, no matter how much teaching style, classroom environment, or peer interactions actually might have played a role, Anthony was always to blame. The fact that he had changed schools five times and behaved differently with structured teachers as opposed to chaotic environments was often overshadowed by explanations that were viewed as more "objective." The hidden story, however, was that the same behavior could be worthy of both recognition and punishment, depending on the perceptions of his copartici-pants. As he got older, the stakes got higher—while in elementary school, punishment might mean his name on the board, in high school, he could be denied valued opportunities that could impact his ability to do what he enjoyed. The catch was, the more he was treated as "the guy who got kicked out of class," the more he became that person.

SOCIAL IMPACT ON STUDENTS' LIVES AND IDENTITIES

Negative perceptions of disability impact not only students' academic learn-ing but their social experiences and relationships with others as well (Davies & Jenkins, 1997). Moving beyond the systemic or school-based issues perpetu-ating disablement, even casual, everyday interactions can send implicit but powerful messages that stereotype and stigmatize students (Olson, 2009). Students interviewed throughout Olson's work describe these interactions as making them "school sick," and feel that they are not fully valued in school due to an aspect of their identity. Even the most well-meaning educators unknowingly can communicate assumptions about students that pigeonhole them into set roles and fixed ability groups, and reinforce these assumptions through the classroom environment itself. Specific examples from Olson's research include a denial of access to learning due to assumptions about the student, tracking based on single testing events or a string of bad grades, or lowering expectations due to struggles with school behavior norms or aca-demic English. Anthony was used to such messages, regularly hearing teach-ers say, "you don't belong here," or anticipating failing grades even before assignments were completed. In Jonathan Mooney's 2007 memoir *The Short Bus,* he similarly describes moments that disabled him, such as when he was banned from using the school bikes because he couldn't follow the lines, tracked into the slow reading group, or even more explicitly, when a teacher publicly yelled, "Jon, what is wrong with you?" Collins's (2013) case study of Jay pointed to physical forms of positioning, where students would have their desks pushed to the outside edges of the class if they were perceived as different. According to these cases (along with others in later chapters of this book), such a restricted view about student potential can result in an inability to take risks, disengagement from learning, and withdrawal from academic activities, or continued underperformance extending to the student's entire school career.

More than anything, stigmatizing perceptions also can lower perfor-mance expectations, exacerbate the school dropout rate for students of color with disabilities, and limit future possibilities to pursue their imagined iden-tities (Wehmeyer, 2008). Even for students without disabilities, traditional schooling often is already perceived as restricting their ability to do real, genuine work because school-based requirements run counter to what they truly love doing (Pope, 2001). When a disconnect between academics and personal goals is compounded by low expectations and messages that belittle the self, the available pathways for students are limited and self-perceptions of value are damaged (Wehmeyer, 2008). Psychologist Robert Kegan (2001) describes this kind of devaluing culture as "toxic" and "dangerous" to the development of adolescent identity because students begin to align themselves with negative perceptions of themselves, which he terms as "a process of self-poisoning." Olson (2009) concurs: "In the supposed meritocracy of schooling, these markers and estimations have profound impact, not just structuring how we fit into the learning hierarchy of an individual classroom, but 'who' we are and whom we believe we will become" (p. 48).

By the time they reach later years in their schooling, it is difficult for students to escape the patterns created by repeated moments of positioning and reputations stemming from being recognized as a certain type of student (Wortham, 2004). Even contrary to beliefs about students labeled as having difficulties reading these social cues, most students are aware of this process and continuously struggle to achieve a sense of connectedness, pass as "normal," and have their strengths recognized by others (Biklen, 2005; Grandin, 1992; Rapley, 2004). While identities are always in motion, they can solidify and "thicken" over months and years (Holland & Lave, 2001), making it extremely difficult for students to erase negative perceptions and reinvent themselves. Even if a student has the opportunity to enter a new setting with different people, the effects of negative beliefs are hard to escape due to the impression made on self-perceptions of ability. In Anthony's case, being removed from five different schools only reinforced the idea that there would always be something wrong with him and that he did not seem to fit anywhere. The primary source of consistency in his school experiences was that he eventually would be excluded and bridges would be burned. While this realization was likely painful in his early years, the high school version of Anthony had built up a dismissive attitude toward schooling that discounted its importance from his long-term vision of his life.

Living and Learning on the Margins

The social construction of disability impacts students' lives in complex ways, which are deeply embedded in both implicit and explicit lessons about what is "normal" (as both modeled and taught in schools). Disability categories themselves articulate the relationship between individual performance and the dividing line between normalcy and disability (Harry et al., 2007). Students in turn learn from how others with perceived differences are treated or whether their status changes in the academic community. Beth Ferri and David Connor (2007) elaborate:

All children come to learn about norms and their own positioning, particularly in relation to others. Thus, classroom walls and more subtle divisions within the classroom act as literal and symbolic borders, assigning students to designated spaces that correspond to their perceived value in society. . . . Social environments such as the classroom create expectations of conformity, and students unable or unwilling to conform to dominant expectations are often relegated to the margins. (p. 130)

In a culture where a sense of belonging is tied to success and achievement, being on the margins can often be associated with stigma and lead to feelings of worthlessness, thus lowering self-esteem (Edgerton, 1993). Labels such as "at risk" reinforce and perpetuate assumptions about what students can and cannot do, and the negative connotations of such terminology continue to be preserved in schools (Keefe, Moore, & Duff, 2006). Shakespeare and Watson (2002) challenge oppressive attitudes of shame that many people with disabilities have toward their impairment, questioning the logic of denying one's own identity in favor of being "ordinary." Similarly, a 20-year longitudinal study by Higgins, Raskind, Goldberg, and Herman (2002) revealed a direct correlation between the participants' levels of success and their understanding and acceptance of their disabilities. At the same time, this research also revealed the long-lasting impact of stigmatizing behavior from adults on students with learning disabilities. Acceptance, therefore, is not always easy to achieve in the face of discouragement and negative attitudes. As Aaron Piziali, who grew up with a learning disability, writes in his life story, "My disability is that I have been disabled, as well as discouraged and discounted by a temporarily able-minded, able-bodied general public. My learning disability is something I must perpetually fight to define and also something I must fight to reject" (Rodis, Garrod, & Boscardin, 2001, p. 31).

Rather than taking a deficit approach to viewing disability as an undesirable state of being, Douglas Biklen (2005) instead argues for the "presumption of competence." This orientation not only implies an optimistic attitude in the face of learning needs but also has concrete implications for classroom practice. While a focus on deficits might result in abandoning efforts to educate or might position the teacher as helpless to make substantial change, presuming competence means that "the teacher is required to turn inward and ask, 'What other approach can I try?'" (p. 72). Anthony, unfortunately, was not always so lucky as to be presumed competent. By the time he reached high school, even the simplest infraction—such as talking out of turn or chatting with his neighbor—would result in dramatic arguments and drastically punitive measures. In school, relationships with peers and adults alike became an inescapably sensitive time bomb, and his every action was always closely monitored and guarded. Anthony pointed out, "[On the debate team] I like being treated more like an intellectual kind of person, not just someone you have to baby-sit like in some of my classes. It helps to get freedom."

The problem of deficit-oriented thinking, however, is that it extends beyond a single teacher and instead is embedded in the complex fabric of human experience. Despite his constant complaints about being labeled with Asperger's as a teenager—"I hate it. I hate that people see me that way."—Anthony himself played a role in perpetuating the negative image he thought others expected of him. Even in debate, for instance, whenever a speech was going "too well," he would deliberately sabotage his participation with jokes to his audience. These moves were initially frustrating to observe because people would rarely look past the jokes to what he actually did well—that is, until we realized that Anthony did not want people to see that far. It was easier for him to continue the self-perpetuating position of the class clown, because at least then the negative attitudes would be directed toward a character he had created, instead of the more vulnerable aspects of his identity. The image of Anthony waiting outside the doorway, greeting students lucky enough to be welcomed in, is paradigmatic of the "water boy" position—not only is he on the outside, but the outsider role itself becomes an official task and job for him to fulfill. The subtle but important difference here is that he is the one who assigns himself this job, as opposed to having people in power require it of him. He alternates between calling himself the "debate water boy" or the "debate bouncer," saying, "I thought the debate team needed one too!"

As opposed to standing idly by while others tell him he does not belong, the move to actively take on this role himself allows him to take some form of control over his positioning in school. Instead of waiting for others to laugh at his speeches, he preempts any laughter by being the one to tell the jokes; if laughter occurs, it is on his own terms. His preemptive efforts are consistent with stereotype threat research by Claude Steele (1997) on self-handicapping, where individuals put up a variety of barriers as a defensive strategy to have something to blame if they fail. In this way, reversing Anthony's cycle would require more than a strengths-based mindset but also focused efforts to address the fear of failure instilled in him as a result of years on the margins of public education.

THE POWER OF SELF-DETERMINATION

Despite the helplessness that the "water boy" image implies, Anthony's case illustrates how adolescents struggle to take ownership over the course of their lives, including even the most negative position. To do so, it is vitally important to be able to have access to the tools and opportunities necessary to regain control over their own lives and counteract pervasive negative external forces. Despite the dire vision of students' life pathways when impacted by disabling practices, students regularly engage in a struggle for control over the course of their lives, and this self-determination is an important factor in identity development. When students can make decisions, set their own goals, and have a sense that their activities serve a broader purpose, they can perceive themselves as able to act successfully in their world (Wehmeyer, 2008). In a 2002 study by Hapner and Imel, for instance, students felt less disenfranchised with schooling when they could voice their concerns and play a role in their IEP process, placement, and other educational decisions. The power of active agency and involvement also helped develop relationships between students and staff, and gave students a precedent for conversation. These findings are consistent with other studies that emphasize the importance of recognition and pride for youth identity and empowerment (Barron & Barron, 1992; Biklen, 2005). In his firsthand account of his experiences with autism, author Sean Barron emphasizes the importance of feeling in control of conversation, stating, "What mattered was that doing it made me feel a little closer to being a normal human being. I got recognition, and I felt powerful for at least a while when I steered the talk where I wanted it to go" (p. 49).

To realize this power and satisfy the innate desire to author his own life, it would not have been enough for Anthony to simply identify himself as an outsider in school. While demonstrating his efforts to exercise agency, in the end, he often had little real control over the demeaning nature of his school experiences. This mattered less in Anthony's case because when this happened, he simply would take solace in his vision of joining the Air Force. Simply having a desire to enter the military would not have been sufficient to actually embark on this journey. Instead, his life outside school offered powerfully consistent validation of his goals as well as opportunities to explore different possibilities related to his path. Growing up in a family with two former members of the military afforded him access to inside knowledge of his desired world, in terms of both formal connections as well as informal conversations at the dinner table. This base knowledge provided him with the foundation to begin researching opportunities on his own, as well as enough background to know which out-of-school opportunities might help develop his skills (such as the Young Marines program and leadership roles in the police shadowing program). Since he perceived school as having almost no role in his ability to pursue this trajectory, the consistently restrictive nature of his academic life mattered less in the bigger picture of his lifelong learning trajectory.

Making Pride Possible

Initially, upon observing the richness of Anthony's efforts to join the military, the research team and I interpreted his actions as an example of how people with disabilities work to "escape" their labels (Smith, 2007). Upon further examination, the notion of escape did not reflect the complex nature of his efforts. It was also misleading because it could be conceived as painting the ableist picture that disability must be "overcome" at all costs (Hehir, 2005). The battle that Anthony waged was instead less about "overcoming" disability and more about regaining control over his life and defining its direction in a way that increased the possibility that he might achieve his dreams. For many others, disability can be a source of pride or even an integral part of a person's culture (Shakespeare, 1996; Shapiro, 1994). In order for pride to be possible, "disability" must be framed as a dimension of identity that is not directly in conflict with deep-seated life goals and pursuits. As the evidence in this chapter has shown, this is not often the case. Instead, students are limited in their chances to feel the sense of accomplishment and personal growth that all people need (Sarason, 1990). Disability becomes "disablement," where negative attitudes and disparaging perceptions restrict what is possible and relegate students to categories that forever position them as outsiders. Students want to align themselves with a vision of "success"—however it is defined in a particular context—and work hard to be seen this way, even at the expense of denying disability as a part of their identity. When it becomes clear that they will never alter people's perceptions, they do what they can to find the experiences and relationships that will expand possibilities for living the life they want to lead and realizing identities they imagine for themselves.

Chapter 2

Ability and the Power of Personal Agency

At 15, Tinsley Hawkins imagined herself as an author, and that came as a surprise to everyone but her. Every day, she would come home to her immaculately organized room and write on her computer for a minimum of 2 hours. She set her favorite pop power songs to the perfect volume (level 5), referenced her copious notes in yellow legal pads, and experimented with different chapter title fonts until she felt ready to begin. It wasn't just the writing that she loved—she felt an almost sentimental joy about being even a small part of the literary world. "My favorite thing about books," she would say, " . . . is just the pages, how they look." Through multicolored books lined up alphabetically on her tidy wall-to-wall bookshelves, she sought both solace and inspiration in the words of Shakespeare, e.e. cummings, Philip Pullman, and Stephanie Meyer. One day, she longed to be able to add her name to that list as a published author. Together with her close group of friends, she imagined fantasy worlds with witches, angels, and colorful adventure quests, passing around a notebook for each girl to add the next chapter. It allowed her to move beyond the daily routine of hiding in a closet or bathroom at home, curled into a ball, remembering her teacher's frustration at how slowly she had done her classwork. It took her past the appointments with school psychologists and endless parent–teacher conferences and special education meetings. Her stories were a secret, hidden from her teachers and from school expectations. She could become an author on her own. As she often said, "I don't think you really write your own stories in school. I don't think they're allowed."

This chapter introduces a mindset for framing how youth resolve tensions in the relationships between how they personally view their capabilities and what others believe about their potential. Instead of conceptualizing "abilities" as a collection of internal traits isolated from the social world, it focuses on ability as a product of the relationship between personal goals and the concerns of others. It describes a framework for examining how students like Tinsley are driven to develop abilities as a way of exerting control over the development of their identities and life directions. Viewing "ability as

33

agency" clarifies how shifts in positioning impact youth participation over time and distinguishes the different ways students resist (Gabel & Peters, 2004) and push back against social constraints. By doing so, it sheds light on the more hidden impacts of disabling practices. Tinsley's case helps illustrate how varying external forces can directly expand or restrict what social psychologist Ole Dreier (2009) terms "scopes of possibility." As Tinsley states in the e.e. cummings quote that introduces Part I of the book, being yourself is "the hardest battle which any human being can fight," particularly when everyone is attempting to make you someone else. According to Tinsley, this means that "first, you have to stop being someone else, then you have to define yourself, then you have to start being that person." Similar to Anthony's struggle, Tinsley's fight involved creating a space where she could safely pursue her image of herself as an author and take ownership of her life.

DEVELOPING AGENCY AND EXPANDING POSSIBILITIES

As psychologist Albert Bandura (2001) articulates, "The capacity to exercise control over the nature and quality of one's life is the essence of humanness" (p. 1). Even simple, everyday decisions are driven by the ever-present quest to create the conditions necessary to achieve personal goals and interests. Agency allows people to intentionally act in the world, take part in their own self-development and adaptation, purposively remake their world, and bring personal significance to their lives (Bandura, 2001; Inden, 1990). These efforts are not exclusively social in nature—the act of influencing and manipulating environmental surroundings also plays a direct role in developing the functional and neuronal structure of the brain (Diamond, 1988; Kolb & Whishaw, 1998). Modifying one's world requires proactive, sustained, and complex struggles that involve foresight, self-monitoring and regulating, planning and goal setting, motivation, and reflective self-reactiveness (Bandura, 1986, 1991, 2001). Exercising agency, then, is directly connected to producing real outcomes that impact a person's life, ideally in a positive way. Bandura (2001) continues, "People adopt courses of action that are likely to produce positive outcomes and discard those that bring unrewarding or punishing outcomes. . . . Agency thus involves the ability to give shape to appropriate courses of action and regulate their execution" (pp. 7–8). In his theory of participation in social practice, Ole Dreier (2009) connects agentic action to the development of ability, arguing that people are driven to develop abilities to expand their power over their opportunities and participation in the world. Rather than the traditional notion of abilities as purely internal properties, Dreier considers how abilities allow people to more freely unfold the direction of their lives and increase control over changing life situations. Examining the development of abilities, he states, allows us to "grasp the ways in which persons develop their properties, modify and change them, and in so doing, change themselves and their world" (p. 33). This process of personal change requires people to figure out what they stand for, identify who supports and who opposes this vision, and discover how they can pursue these dreams across the many experiences they encounter.

For students, school is a place intended to help develop such abilities, fostering the experiences necessary to pursue their goals, expand their access to future opportunities, and succeed in the real world. At the same time, school itself is also a context where there is a range of what is possible for students, depending on their past histories, relations with others, and whether they meet the expectations of the school culture. Dreier (2009) refers to this concept as "scopes of possibilities," where different contexts offer people more or less control over their lives, depending on whether the actions available to them are restricted or far-reaching. A student who is celebrated for his academic success, for instance, may be encouraged by his teachers to enroll in advanced placement courses and summer enrichment, allowing him to exert greater command over his goal to become a successful attorney. The public-speaking and research abilities he wants to develop to achieve this goal are available and possible in the school context, and these abilities give him the capacity to make decisions about the direction of his life. In this way, possessing relevant abilities expands what is possible in a context, increasing individual agency.

While there are external forces and opportunities that help support an individual's quest to pursue desired life directions, there are also incidents that threaten it. The scope of what is possible for a student is inherently governed by the circumstances that student has to address in order to achieve his or her goals. Claude Steele calls these factors "identity contingencies," referring to the unique issues and potential issues people have to deal with due to the nature of their social identity in a given situation. In his book, *Whistling Vivaldi and Other Clues to How Stereotypes Affect Us*, Steele (2010) argues identity contingencies can constrain people's actions both by restricting access to valued opportunities and by "putting a threat in the air" of living under the cloud of damaging assumptions. Negative stereotypes related to an aspect of a person's identity can increase her awareness of the stereotype and subsequent fear of fulfilling it, jeopardizing her performance and development of important abilities related how she wants to live her life. The same student who wanted to become a successful attorney might be perceived as unable to develop public-speaking abilities and prevented from joining the debate team because of his learning disability. Even if the opportunity to join the team was available to him, the mere threat of fulfilling the assumption that students with learning disabilities are incapable of succeeding in debate might impact his performance. In both cases, external forces and identity contingencies have the power to restrict his development of desired abilities.

Influential Power Relations

Negative stereotypes also are tied to social status and power relations that influence this process, as they impact the rights people have in a particular setting as well as their freedom to participate (Harré, 1983). The right to act is a fundamental means through which people find meaning in their lives, but individual action often is met with interpersonal power struggles that are not without turmoil. This is especially the case when people are positioned in a way that is not aligned with how they view themselves. As Harré argues in his theory of social positioning, the dynamic nature of social interaction lends itself to subtle patterns distributing what people are allowed (and entitled) to say or do (Harré & Slocum, 2003). The broader institutional context underlying these actions drives the nature of positioning and consequent participation. Shifts in positioning also can occur and mingle across diverse contexts, directly impacting individual participation, possibilities for action, and identity formation. Even so, in every context, there is someone whose position means that his or her participation will be restricted. According to Harré and Slocum (2003), "Does everyone have equal access to the local repertoire of meaningful actions? Surely not. Some members of a group are more advantageously positioned than others. Some categories of persons are more advantageously positioned" (p. 124). When a student with a disability is negatively perceived by those around him, he can be restricted in his access to valued opportunities that might be related to abilities he would like to develop in relation to personal goals. Even when supports are in place, social attitudes toward him can forever place him in boxes marked with assumptions about future behavior, like "the one who goofs off all the time," "the one who can't spell," "the one who doesn't try," "the one who must be supervised." Such labels can further disable people, positioning them as unable to make the changes necessary to fully participate. In light of research on human agency, this is especially significant because restricted action can mean a limited scope of possibility and a lack of control over the nature and quality of one's life, "the essence of humanness."

TINSLEY AND SCHOOL

Tinsley's early years in school quickly set her on a path to restricted participation. While she had always loved books and storytelling with her family growing up, she had difficulty learning to read. For her mother Adelle, it was heartbreaking to watch her young daughter work so hard and fall increasingly further behind. Despite her timid nature, Tinsley was ambitious, and would feel stupid when she could see that she was not able to do what other students were doing. According to Adelle, "Her big thing was that she just didn't want people to think she was stupid, and so over time, her way of dealing with it was to be very, very quiet, and preparation was the name of the game." As the years went by, observed limitations mounted up from her teachers, parents, and psychologists. Her kindergarten teacher worried that Tinsley might have a visual perception issue when she could not identify shapes, and her parents worried Tinsley could not pronounce "r" and "l" sounds, would reverse letters, and read from right to left. Psychologists recommended a speech and language therapist, and found that she had a visual perception disability and auditory processing issues. Their evaluation concluded that it was difficult for Tinsley to recognize the correct orientation of objects and resulted in an IEP to provide occupational therapy (for visual perception) and speech therapy.

Despite the multiple layers of worry and abundance of explanations for why Tinsley could not perform successfully in school, she continued to feel increasingly more helpless over her situation. In our interviews, Tinsley remembered feeling especially traumatized in 4th grade, when she had a teacher who would become easily frustrated by students who did not grasp material quickly. The IEP supports mattered little in the face of how she felt when she was unable to answer discussion questions as rapidly as other students, and there was no other recourse but to withdraw socially. Adelle recalls seeing Tinsley come home every day from school and lie on the floor, curled up in the fetal position. Hiding in the closet became a regular routine to gain some semblance of peace at the end of the day. It did not come as a surprise when Tinsley's speech showed no improvement with the twice weekly, 30-minute sessions of speech therapy from the school district in addition to the private therapist she was seeing. As it turned out, for Tinsley, the damage she experienced in school was less about the diagnoses and labels themselves. Instead, it was more about constantly feeling like success would always be impossible for her, given how she was being treated at school.

Feeling Safe and Developing Writing Abilities

Although Tinsley was constantly under observation, few people beyond her parents knew that she was deeply creative and had started putting together original plays with her neighbor at age 9. Her active imagination rarely had a place in school, until she transferred to a private K–8 school in 5th grade. The project-driven and artistic activities spoke to Tinsley, who even began to enjoy public speaking and debates in class. She quickly found a close group of friends, one of whom was an avid writer. Together, they would write fantasy stories, taking turns writing chapters and trading back and forth over the course of the year. For Tinsley, these friendships created a safe place to foster their common interests where "it did not matter that we weren't part of the popular group at school." Today, Tinsley bashfully admits that she thinks of herself as an expert writer. During the first home visit, she showed me some of the early sketches of one of her 140-page novels.

> RESEARCHER: What is an expert writer? What does it take?
> TINSLEY: Passion, I guess. But you have to be really creative and have a lot of ideas, and be able to write. Not something you can be taught, it's something you just know how to do. You're born with it.
> RESEARCHER: Were you born with it?
> TINSLEY: I guess. I don't know. Maybe.
> RESEARCHER: How often do you write? Do you write every day?
> TINSLEY: I try to do it at least once every other day. A chapter a day.
> RESEARCHER: A chapter a day? Are you putting together a book?
> TINSLEY: Yes.
> RESEARCHER: How long have you been working on it?
> TINSLEY: Since 8th grade.
> RESEARCHER: Oh wow, so it's a big project then.
> TINSLEY: Yeah, I'm almost done with my second book.
> RESEARCHER: Does anyone read them?
> TINSLEY: My mom has read some stuff, but they're just for fun. Maybe one day I'll send them somewhere.
> RESEARCHER: How long are these?
> TINSLEY: On my computer, they're only like 140 pages.
> RESEARCHER: Per book.
> TINSLEY: Yes.
> RESEARCHER: Typewritten?
> TINSLEY: Yeah.
> RESEARCHER: That's impressive! I should have you write my book for me! (laughter) So what do you want to be after high school? Is writing going to play a big role in that, do you think?
> TINSLEY: I want to be a writer, but I want to be realistic too, so I want to try something else along with writing, you know? Because realistically, there are very few writers who actually make it.

The extent of Tinsley's writing practices only solidified her belief that they ran counter to what school valued and required. Although her middle school experience provided her with the confidence to pursue her interest in writing, Tinsley chose to keep her true passions separate from school, where the perceived risk of sharing her work was too great.

> RESEARCHER: Do you think that what you're learning right now will be useful for becoming a writer? Is there a connection between your English classes and being a writer?

TINSLEY: It's not very useful. There's a connection but it's not that useful. It's more about spelling and stuff. And if I was a writer, I mean,
there would be people to check it.

RESEARCHER: Do any teachers ever read your stuff?

TINSLEY: (Shakes head vigorously)

RESEARCHER: No. So this is not anything you ever do for school?

TINSLEY: No.

RESEARCHER: How come?

TINSLEY: I don't think it really goes into the criteria, like English, you
know? And the short stories we have to write, I'm not good at that
stuff because they have to be really long for me.

RESEARCHER: How come?

TINSLEY: I don't know. Because I'll get an idea and it starts off kind of
short, but that idea isn't really good, so I'll get another idea and it's
longer, and then . . . I keep getting all these ideas but they would
only work for that one story. And so it like, expands.

RESEARCHER: So what is your writing like in school then?

TINSLEY: Um, I can do the essays short, which is usually what happens in
school. And that's usually all you have to do in school. I don't think
you really write your own stories in school.

As Tinsley states, none of her teachers (particularly in high school) were
aware of her novels or creative writing although they would describe her as
diligent and hardworking. Standardized state tests continued to reveal lower
scores in writing mechanics, concepts, and skills. During observations in high
school English and French classes, we would see a version of Tinsley that
always turned in her work but did not stand out. She stayed below the radar,
saying that English class was less about creativity or coming up with the most
interesting ideas, and more about doing the work. She could be a writer on
her own time, on her own terms.

Tinsley is not alone in living her life in many diverse ways, navigating
the borders of "multiple worlds" governed by varying values and norms
(Phelan, Davidson, & Cao, 1991). As William James writes, "We may prac-
tically say that he has as many different social selves as there are distinct
groups of persons about whose opinion he cares. He generally shows a
different side of himself to each of these different groups" (quoted in Goffman, 1959, p. 48). An important aspect of the "ability as agency" framework is that personal change and development often occur while we are
making sense of the contradictions of life (Dreier, 2009). The challenge is
to somehow resolve the tensions that interfere with the life we want and to
make sense of the contradictions of life while avoiding its complete collapse
in the process.

DIFFERENT PLACES, DIFFERENT POWERS, DIFFERENT STAKES

While it would be simpler to dismiss Tinsley's writing practices as a mere hobby with less relevance in the classroom, her diverse forms of participation instead can be attributed to agency. Bandura (2001) concurs:

> Through agentic action, people devise ways of adapting flexibly to remarkably diverse geographic, climatic and social environments; they figure out ways to circumvent physical and environmental constraints, redesign and construct environments to their liking, create styles of behavior that enable them to realize desired outcomes, and pass on the effective ones to others by social modeling and other experimental modes of influence. By these inventive means, people improve their odds in the fitness survival game. (p. 22)

Tinsley is not alone in her efforts to navigate varying environmental constraints, as most social contexts are already set up and institutionalized to channel certain kinds of participation from certain individuals, depending on their positioning (Dreier, 2009). Schools in particular often are arranged to promote certain tracks and pathways for different types of students (Oakes, 2005). The specific skills and abilities required in a context, along with the values of their coparticipants and people in power, bring about different forms of participation from each person. At the same time, even in the face of social positioning, there is still room for self-authoring (Holland et al., 1998; Wortham, 2006). Even with actions situated in broader cultural phenomena, people continue to struggle for control over their actions (Holland & Leander, 2004).

As Tinsley experienced, the self-authoring process can be quite delicate, given that there are "very different things at stake for persons in different contexts and their personal concerns vary significantly across them" (Dreier, 2009, p. 196). Individual actions, decisions, and goals are continuously driven by a desire to preserve what personally matters most, as well as to produce desirable results, escape social "enslavement," and avoid outcomes that might endanger these concerns (Bandura, 1991; Feather, 1982; Locke & Latham, 1990; Vygotsky, 1993). Over time, people begin to embrace entire identities that revolve around participation in the activities they care most deeply about (Nasir & Cooks, 2009). These "practice-linked identities" in turn are related to engagement and a feeling of connection that inspires even more intense activity (Nasir & Cooks, 2009). Unique identities also develop as people continually redefine how they imagine themselves in relation to others (Lave & Wenger, 1991; Wortham, 2004). As with Tinsley's writing group, participation is further driven by the desire to seek membership in communities with common intentions (Wenger, 1998). All of these layers of resources contribute to the more long-term process of the "thickening" of a student's identity (Holland & Lave, 2001; Wortham, 2006). Since the power to pursue personal desires is such an integral feature of identity and the development of personal agency, it is important to facilitate the process of developing the abilities that will help students realize possibilities. This is consistent with Vygotsky's (1993) work highlighting the importance of providing opportunities for children to learn and explore their unrealized potential in creative ways with the support of an adult.

Although Tinsley's mother insisted that she was rarely allowed to read Tinsley's manuscripts, she was one of many key influences on the development of Tinsley's abilities. As an attorney working largely from home, Adelle modeled the same work practices that Tinsley took on for her own writing. Together after school, they would go to their private workspaces, complete with identical piles of yellow legal pads. Tinsley's entire family also positioned Tinsley as having the right to her creative freedom, giving her the space to pursue her writing without the pressure of having to publicly display it. Other social supports included the aforementioned writing group of close friends, in addition to the writing mentors and expanded writing network she acquired at a summer writing program on an out-of-state college campus. Tinsley's own disciplined practices also tied her to the writer identity. As a natural observer, she prided herself on paying close attention to the world around her, taking care to note potential popular media influences. Famous authors and characters were always present during the writing process, both through her copious memorization of useful quotes and colored tabs she put in books to mark passages that inspired her with description, character development, or witty dialogue. She continued to preserve the distinction from school by using the computer for her writing and handwriting her schoolwork—despite the many external influences on her ability development, she did not perceive school as one of them.

THE THREAT OF DISABLEMENT

It was important that Tinsley had so many outside sources positioning her as a writer and supporting her power to pursue this goal. Although she never expressed great pride in her disability, she did not identify it as restricting her available possibilities. Disability did not have to mean "the loss or limitation of opportunities to take part in the life of the community on an equal level with others" (Burchardt, 2004, p. 736) or "an oppressive relationship between people with impairments and the rest of society" (Finkelstein, 1980, p. 47).

Having a safe space where the disability aspect of her social identity was not a threat to her goals mattered in terms of her efforts to pursue them. These supports also played a significant role in developing her ability to set goals and foresee ways to further those goals (such as seeking out the summer writing program). Foresight is an integral skill enabling people to transcend the dictates of their immediate environment in productive ways (Bandura, 2001)— lacking opportunities to develop it leaves them trapped and unable to pursue something new. If students are negatively positioned, under threat of negative stereotypes, and there are no supportive experiences to develop foresight and encourage agency, they are put at a disservice both in terms of achieving their personal goals and building the capacity to improve their lives.

But what, if any, risks might there be in Tinsley's perception that school had little to no role in her development as a writer? Although both the Anthony and Tinsley cases show students who exercise their agency in spaces outside of school, this is not to say that being disconnected from school in the face of disabling practices is the ultimate solution. In fact, fragmenting one's life so completely can potentially lead to missed opportunities or experiences that actually might further the development of relevant abilities. Placing so much reliance on independent efforts can put students at greater risk in case their vision is not realized. Such a disconnect also can cause a student to be viewed as "unmotivated" or disengaged, or even lead to poor academics, all of which can contribute to the further restriction of a student's agency.

The problem is greater than single individuals, who cannot singlehandedly reverse the debilitating impacts of disablement. As Oliver and Barnes (1998) argue, "If the barriers to full participation are not intrinsic to the individual but rather are social in nature, it is a matter of social justice that these barriers should be dismantled" (as cited in Burchardt, 2004, p. 736). The stakes are high if this does not happen, particularly over time when students' identities become objectified in stable, predictable ways that can restrict their agency (Lemke, 2000; Wortham, 2008). This is easier said than done, especially when "it is concerned with revealing the explicit and implicit patterns of reasoning that are realized in the ways that people act towards others" (Harré, Moghaddam, Cairnie, Rothbart, & Sabat, 2009). In this way, positions also can be linked to cultural stereotypes and deeply embedded assumptions about the meaning and value of different types of behavior. How people act toward one another in ways that impact their positioning must be understood in the context of life, including the "abiding inclinations, needs, and wants of the person engaging in that behavior" (Harré & Moghaddam, 2003, p. 92). Making sense of the positioning process requires not only an understanding of individual motives but also attention to the cultural assumptions and expectations that govern behavior.

Hazardous Trajectories of Ability

While Tinsley continues to be able to pursue her path toward becoming a writer, her story could have had a completely different outcome if she had encountered powerful academic stereotypes or had been unable to move out from underneath the shadow of oppressive academic histories. As her case demonstrates, the development of personal abilities and manifestation of disability are both deeply social matters that are driven by issues of positioning and possibility. As people go through life, they are compelled to develop abilities to expand their control over their own lives and direct their pathways according to what matters most to them. They do not act in isolation, and how a person's life unfolds is realized through positioned relations with countless others. This kind of research must account for participation across contexts as well as pay attention to cultural and historical resources that empower or constrain identity formation (Penuel & Wertsch, 1995). To better account for the ways in which people develop abilities to expand their power over their lives, there must be a clearer examination of the intersections between personal goals and the concerns of others in different contexts. Understanding the varying scopes of possibilities that are even available as individuals exercise their agency also requires attention to the power dynamics, social positioning, and personal and institutional histories at play in the process of ability development. Given these social forces influencing the development of ability as agency, analysis must attend to:

- the concerns of the individual;
- the prior participation and histories of the individual;
- the concerns of coparticipants;
- positioning and status of the individual in relation to what others can do (along with what that position means in context);
- contextual arrangements and the scope of possibilities for the individual in that context; and
- tensions between the existing social practice and what the individual desires.

If students are to succeed in changing their situations and realizing their goals, it is important to address the nature and structure of social relations within the learning environment itself. Framing learning experiences as opportunities to develop abilities relevant to personal goals, and offering choices with which to explore them can help facilitate more agentic actions (Harpur, 2012; Rabiee & Glendinning, 2010). Most important, students must be taught how to consider the relationship between their concerns and intentions and those of others around them (Dreier, 2009). The process of resolving inherent contradictions that happen to interfere with personal goals requires a complex understanding of other people, which also must be taught. Realizing personal possibilities cannot take place in isolation and requires working with others, appreciating their differences, and understanding what lies beneath the surface. As Tinsley aptly states at the conclusion of one interview, "I like things that seem really simple but they're really complicated. That's what I like about human beings. They seem so predictable and so human, and really, really simple, you know? But we're really actually complicated underneath."

Part II

DISABLING PRACTICES AND YOUTH RESISTANCE

Being pulled out of class almost every day for 3 years affected me in many ways. I felt as if I was not smart enough and I felt that people thought I was 'dumb' and not capable of learning what they were learning. When you are put down and told that you can't do something, you put up this wall, this barrier to not get hurt.

—Ana Martinez, 16

A Mother's Tale

Just as schoolchildren innocently speculate that their teachers sleep at school, extensive time spent with a person in one place can easily contribute to the illusion of total understanding about the other parts of their lives. I took comfort in the patterns that were beginning to form with regard to Anthony's participation at school, luring me with the assurance that I soon would be able to draw conclusions about his life. From debate class to English and math classes, I documented his carefully crafted persona at school, where he alternated between chatting with people around him to telling jokes to the class. Teacher reactions ranged from pure exasperation to barely concealed smiles at his stories. He was the proverbial class clown.

But surprises abound in the face of complacency. The Anthony who greeted us at the door of his home during our first visit asked for our coats, escorted us to the dining room, and responded to his parents with a practiced, "Yes, ma'am," and "No, sir." As he took us on a tour of his house, the class clown transformed into the bookworm and collector. He eagerly led us through his binder of military badges, coin collection, complete with a Marine Corps silver dollar, assortment of military helmets he purchased at an antiques store, and the place on the wall where he planned to hang a Swiss flag celebrating his ancestry. As he regaled us with detailed descriptions of his past and current goals for the future, we were surrounded with models of Air Force One, helicopters, miniature police cars purchased in Switzerland, and his freshly pressed uniform from Young Marines. While the nerf gun, basketball hoop in the backyard, and even the bulletproof vest from his police shadowing program came as less of a surprise, we weren't prepared for the bookshelves. The floor-to-ceiling towers were crammed with sophisticated selections, from general volumes on world wars, Egypt, and Russia, to biographies of more obscure military figures, interspersed with posted pictures of him with friends in Young Marines. The bottom of his nightstand was overflowing with political periodicals and news magazines, and in the midst of it all, his boot camp graduation photo. He wistfully described the first book he ever finished, the *World War II Encyclopedia* he got for his 8th birthday. Although there was a World War II class offered at school, he scoffed at the idea of taking it because he didn't think the teacher would tolerate his behavior. After closing down the computer tabs containing links to the jobs he wanted to pursue in the Air Force, he shook his head and dismissed it all, saying, "I'm obviously too obsessed with this stuff and have no life. I enjoy hanging out with friends, but the problem is I've got my home life and my school life."

Later on, over an immaculate spread of fruit salad, homemade brownies, and afternoon tea, his mother Greta recounted yet another dimension of Anthony's history. She lowered her already soft-spoken voice in case Anthony was listening from his homework post in the next room, and launched into her story.

We always had books around, we didn't skimp on those. Early on, he would sit there and flip through them—he got to choose the book and we always read to him, every night, many, many books. He always enjoyed that and it was nice for us too. I used to be concerned for him as a kid because he would keep looking at encyclopedias and catalogues about animals and I would say, "Don't you want to read a storybook?" He quickly got bored with the stories we read, because he wanted the encyclopedias and the magazines we got, like *Time* and *Newsweek.*

No matter what happened in school with his behavior and test performance, his love for books and reading stayed constant. But as he got older, he would get in trouble because he would be in class and he was supposed to be listening and he'd pull out a book. And I learned that this was a compensatory mechanism for him, he was trying to deal so much with teachers and what was going on inside him and trying to keep himself in equilibrium. And he got in trouble for that, which was understandable, but now we know what books meant to him. At the time, though, we would use it as a punishment: "You're not doing your homework, you can't read!" And we hated to do it, but there were times we had to . . . (laughs) I mean, what is wrong with us, we're taking away books? . . . "gimme all your books." I mean, he had a stack in his bathroom, he had them all over.

In grade school, he always tested well above average and then in 4th grade, it started coming down. I kept asking the people at school what was wrong, and they kept telling me he was lazy, he wasn't working up to his potential. I hate that phrase. They'd say, he's GATE [Gifted and Talented Education], he shouldn't be having these problems and I was like, "Why is he doing this?" When he was young he was just so open and inquisitive and . . . I have a picture of him where it is raining and I put him in his slicker and he's like (mimes picking something up), "worms!" And you could see his bright light and he's got his little yellow galoshes and his slicker and he's got a worm and he's just so happy. He went from scoring almost at the top and then there was a drastic change and it kept going down.

He knew he was getting into trouble in 4th grade and in 5th grade things just fell off the rails and he'd start saying, "Well, I'm not good at math." I could tell he was trying to figure out what was going on, and he was so depressed. I know it affected him and it caused a lot of grief. He would hear me say, "In 4th grade this . . . in 5th grade that . . . ," and he would start parroting me. But see, I was advocating for him, but then he heard that and made it a reason why, looking for an explanation for it all. And the first thing he would use to describe himself would be to say he didn't like school.

Every year it starts out, he's enthusiastic, and we think, "Oh, wow, things are going to be better," and then it comes crashing down and around April or March, it's the same thing and I'm not surprised, you know? There's still highs and lows. He is flunking math and we had this big conference last week. His big thing was that he didn't want anyone helping him, he wanted to do it himself. But then I find out he hasn't been turning in his homework, his classwork, he's falling asleep in class, and now he has to bring up his grade by Friday. So they said, well, he can drop out . . . but what are we teaching him? He needs to persevere and sometimes he's just going to have to get an F. We tried to tell him that it wouldn't look good on his transcript, even if he went into the military. Sometimes, he does better, but he alienates himself in class with some of his behaviors, especially in math. His dad would try to get him to help with the house and stuff, and he'll say, "Well, I don't like to work," but he'll do it for other people and he'll do it for a job. We tried to teach him some geometry things related to it and he would be real resistant. I didn't know whether it was just something new, or. . . . You know, we tell him, you really have a good sense of humor, you should do something with it! But he doesn't talk about anything else that he is good at . . . the military is his thing. He structures himself and learns about the military in his free time. And there have never been any behavior issues at Young Marines. Because it is structured. In the military, it is more black and white, and when you fall out of line, there's consequences. So that's kind of what we use now: Well, you're doing this, what do you think is going to happen in the military if you do this? We use that analogy. And he gets bored with too much freedom. He'll say he wants it, but then he'll say, "I'm bored, I don't have anything to do." And school is not structured for a kid like this. We thought about sending him to a special school, but I think the kids there are a lot more symptomatic than Anthony. Sometimes I'm not sure if he has Asperger's or if he is just somewhere on the spectrum or what, but at this point it doesn't matter that much. When they first came up with something I was so glad, because at least it wasn't just me being told there was nothing wrong. He didn't see it as a comfort; it was more for me and trying to get services in school because otherwise he wouldn't. But still with things he doesn't like, he'll still pull out a book, read, or talk to somebody else.

But I think now he's starting to feel more positive about himself. He is really enthusiastic about going to debate and there are other programs that made a big difference. We wanted him to do a lot more when he was younger, but he would say, "No, no, I don't want to do it." The problem we had was that if he didn't want to do something, he'd misbehave, so rather than push him and deal with all those behavior issues, it was better just to keep him in the same kinds of things. And it is hard because his social circles vary and I don't think they're consistent and he'll get negatively viewed by people. But I think he has a great sense of humor, and I think he's caring. He can be real serious, especially when he talks to adults, he can be a great kid. He even advises the cops on different weaponry and they ask him about it because he knows that stuff. So they talk to him and they talk about the real world.

It has been so hard, you know? What do you do? We want to keep him on the right path so much. It's been really hard, because even as parents, we kind of pulled in too, because if your kid has a problem, people make judgments. I remember even in the beginning with the debate parents' meetings, I wasn't sure whether I should go because it's hard because you don't know what the parents know, and the perceptions and you know, it's like you guard yourself against that because it's your kid. I was often in the position where I felt like I was the only advocate for him, especially in grade school against other adults, like other educators. And there were a few people who have been really incredible who talk to him so nicely, telling him like it was, but really in a positive way I thought, so I have been really appreciative. He's lucky in that there are a few major mentors in his life, who talk to him like he needs it and are very straight with him. Anyone who spends time and talks to him instead of talking at him. You know, I used to be a proponent for public education but now I don't know anymore with Anthony's experience. I've learned a lot, learned an awful lot.

After Greta finished her tale, the conversation turned to happier moments, like the family trip they had taken recently to Switzerland and family outings to the beach. Anthony came back into the house from playing basketball and his father arrived home from work, and we all settled down to lasagna and desserts that comforted the soul. Anthony suggested a Friday movie night and selected *My Boy Jack*, a World War I film about Rudyard Kipling, to which everyone enthusiastically agreed. As everyone settled in to their favorite seats and the family Dalmatian mix snored beside them, it was a serene interlude in the midst of the traumatic stories of disappointment, frustration, blame, and regret. When it was over, we packed up our equipment and Anthony stayed in his seat, quietly thumbing through a book for fun, instead of as a shield.

Chapter 3

Stereotypes and Restricted Trajectories of Learning

No matter how hard they fight, personal legacies of social marginalization lead some young people to buy in to stereotypes and internalize the belief that they are intellectually inferior to others. Disparaging side comments and looks from adults, laughter from their peers, and rigid definitions of academic success make it difficult to contradict the expectations of failure—that they are "retarded," "that school is a prison camp," or that "teachers see me as a lost hope" (Spencer). The more their intelligence is challenged, the tougher they have to become. Despite the hard exterior, in their more vulnerable moments young people tell stories that embody the notion that human intelligence is fragile and deeply tied to relations with others around them (Postman, 1988). Prejudice and racism may be officially unacceptable, but research has long established evidence of how pervasive and subtle stereotypes can be (Brophy & Good, 1974; Weinstein, 2002). Studies by Joshua Aronson and Claude Steele (2005) point to the unintentional and nonverbal process of stereotyping, and how the simple awareness of stereotypes can bias perceptions of ability, even among people who reject them. Assumptions about capabilities also have been embedded in the very structure of schooling itself through uneven responses to student behavior and academic performance, which often appear in practices that single out or isolate certain students (Dyson, 1994). Young people notice and internalize implicit and explicit messages about the significance of certain human differences and patterns related to race and gender (Nasir & Hand, 2008; Noguera, 2003; Tyson, 2003). For adolescents seeking a sense of belonging among their peers and hoping to achieve what they imagine from their lives, having aspects of their identities treated as a barrier to acceptance has dire consequences. The message behind such disabling practices is not subtle: It is not always okay to "be yourself."

This chapter examines the presence of academic stereotypes and the long-term consequences of negative social positioning on the learning, identity development, and life directions of young people. Since beliefs about personal capabilities are directly related to a range of interactions with other people, it primarily considers the values and beliefs of educators and students' peer groups, in addition to the school settings and home lives. It pays special attention to peer influence, in light of the heightened need for acceptance from other students that arises in adolescence (Noguera, 2003; Phelan, Davidson, & Yu, 1998; Steinberg, 1996). The discussion elaborates on the "scopes of possibilities" dimension of the framework to explore how social relations can directly impact students' trajectories of participation, particularly in the face of stereotypes that restrict what is possible for them. I use two cases of students who were on the same debate team as Anthony Gustafson and branch off into their lives to show how they were limited by assumptions based on race and past academic histories. The debate context provided a useful setting because it was inherently interactive and required students to verbally articulate and defend their passions, interests, and beliefs in a competitive context. At the same time, it was tied to presumptive beliefs about intelligence that traditionally confine team membership to the academic elite. The cases of Spencer MacArthur and Devin Foster help illustrate how young people continue to develop abilities in places where they are told that they do not belong.

SPENCER ON PROBATION

By the time he entered high school, Spencer MacArthur was already positioned as a troublemaker and generally was tracked into lower academic classes other than English. While many 9th-graders take advantage of the transition to high school as a chance to reinvent themselves, Spencer was constantly under the shadow of two unfortunate incidents that occurred at the end of 8th grade. He first was caught carrying a paper bag of marijuana to a waiting car after being asked by an older student to do so. A few weeks later, he was caught bringing a BB gun to school, a second offense that landed him in criminal court, where he was sentenced to 6 months of probation. His family was shocked by the harsh nature of the sentencing and was quickly thrown into a world filled with meetings, hearings, and endless paperwork. Struggling to find sympathy and support during the early stages of the court process, his father sought the help of a psychologist who diagnosed Spencer as having attention deficit hyperactivity disorder (ADHD). While the psychologist initially was doubtful about the diagnosis and described Spencer as "borderline," he was subsequently convinced by the history of ADHD in the family and descriptions of Spencer's impulsive nature. According to Spencer's mother, "There was a lot of impetus to get him diagnosed because we were facing going to court. The psychologist said 25% of incarcerated juveniles are ADHD and to be careful." On top of his court struggles and getting used to the physical effects of his new medication, Spencer wrestled with the diagnosis because it meant that "people look at you and think you're 'that,' they label you." The disability diagnosis added yet another layer to his already complicated identity, being an adopted Caucasian boy in a Japanese American family with a Japanese brother who also was adopted. Even before these events, he had already been wrestling with his racial identification and recently had been describing himself as a "redneck" and asserting his pride in being White. Being diagnosed with ADHD in high school was an unexpected addition to his social identification, accompanied by a host of negative contingencies.

The court proceedings took up the entirety of Spencer's first year of high school, limiting the time he had for activities other than court-sanctioned community service. The terms of his probation prevented him from attending many overnight debate tournaments, despite spending countless hours working on debate after school, performing well at local tournaments, and completing the work necessary to attend. He fought to continue his reputation as a champion swimmer and county record holder, even when his medication compromised his drive and energy. During that year, he maintained his involvement on both the debate and swimming teams, with the help of supportive coaches whom he respected and viewed as mentors, as opposed to most adults, whom he had little patience for. Unfortunately, by the end of the year, both his swim coach and debate coach, Andrew Lee, coincidentally left the school at the same time. Spencer already had a history of being more outspoken or defiant with teachers he did not like, and it was only a few months before he quit both teams. He pulled away from further involvement with the school. Spencer instead devoted himself wholeheartedly to multiplayer video games such as Call of Duty and Medal of Honor, which he would, at several points, play for over 22 consecutive hours.

By the time the court proceedings were finished, it was the middle of Spencer's sophomore year, and he had already solidified his reputation as someone who did not care about school. He was still enrolled in honors English, but constantly felt victimized by the teacher, who refused to accept his work if there was even the slightest mistake. In an interview with his teacher, she described him as "trouble" and would say, "This is advanced English, and he does not belong here." With teachers whom Spencer described as "nicer," he reasoned, "Well, they just see me as a lost hope who just doesn't try," as opposed to someone who was "retarded," as he believed other teachers viewed him. The same rhetoric was echoed in statements from his peers, which Spencer also noticed. His debate teammates described him as someone who "just didn't want to learn" and attributed blame for his unhappy school life to his lack of effort. According to Natalie, one of his peers on the Hillside debate team:

School can be inspiring, but you have to make it inspiring for yourself. You have to seek out what really floats your boat. If you're not the kind of person who seeks it out, then school is not inspiring and you get Fs. Like with Spencer, if he can't find something he likes because he's not that kind of person, obviously nothing is going to change for him and it's his fault.

Regardless of whether he was accepted by his teammates, Spencer wistfully reflected on his time in debate. While he did not miss "arguing with stupid people and losing," he missed his debate coach. He would point specifically to the academic support he received with math assignments and debate speeches, and the personal support he got when Andrew would make sure he ate, despite his lack of appetite due to the ADHD medication. Spencer continued:

I won't come back to debate unless he does. It wasn't debate I liked, but him as a person. He knew how to push the right buttons, and gave me time to finish my work and was chill. He never made the work stressful or let it completely engulf you, and he believed in what he was saying. Other classes, the work is just useless . . . and it's not even accepting of other people. My other teacher, she won't accept you because you aren't up to a certain level. He used to get diverse groups to work, and debate was unique that way. You didn't have to sit quietly, you're allowed to argue and it's fun to do when you're actually doing it.

In contrast, Spencer remained surrounded by messages from peers and adults reminding him of the threat of being "retarded." Even when statements about being stupid were not directly addressed to him, the learning environment itself often would contain phrases emphasizing the importance of being intelligent. The following interaction, for instance, commonly would occur in Spencer's band class in response to any negative behavior.

STUDENT A: (stacking trumpet mutes on Student B's head, instead of looking at the music, while Spencer looks on and laughs)
TEACHER: (to the student) Go take your medicine or something! I'm pretty sure you haven't! That was retarded! That was a 7th-grade move!
STUDENT B: You don't have to call someone out on something like that, that's so rude!
TEACHER: Be more mature then!
STUDENT B: That's so rude.
TEACHER: Sorry I hurt your feelings, boohoo!

In response to situations like the above, Spencer would shrug nonchalantly, dismissing it as just "part of getting through the day," because at school, "you don't get respect," "you don't get to pinpoint what you need in life," and "you don't get to feel a sense of accomplishment." He continued one more year in high school and then left after passing his GED, enjoying his new job at a hardware store and hoping to pursue his long-time goal of entering the Marines.

THE SHADOW OF PERSONAL HISTORIES

As William Faulkner (1950) once wrote, "The past is never dead. It's not even past" (p. 73). Over the course of his early high school years, Spencer continued to be haunted by two threatening shadows of the past: his own adolescent truancy and the ever-present institutional stereotype of the unmotivated student. Regardless of his triumphs in debate and swimming, his self-perception of being someone who "just doesn't care about school" and his peers' and teachers' perceptions of him as someone who "does not belong" soon became his dominant identity. The more complex dynamics of his adolescent history were taken for granted, such as the social ramifications of being on probation and the fact that he received a diagnosis of ADHD that was associated by trained professionals with delinquency and incarceration. After the court process concluded, Spencer's negative reputation and self-image as a troublesome student remained. He continued to be placed in lower track classes and was surrounded with disabling messages about being a lost hope or the threat of being considered "retarded." The twisted nature of these dynamics was that Spencer remained the singular focus of blame, with even his peers parroting the same judgment as teachers—if he was having an unhappy time in school, he was at fault. Even Spencer himself could see that he would always be someone who was not accepted at school, given that he did not fit into the socially accepted behaviors of working quickly, doing what he was told, staying quiet, and being focused. He even had the diagnosis to prove it.

The idea that academic failure is a cultural fact and extends beyond the perceived faults and qualities of individual students is well-established in academic literature (Henry, 1963; McDermott, 1993; Reid & Valle, 2004; Varenne & McDermott, 1998). Unfortunately, in practice, stereotypes about students based on past behavior and performance continue to dominate their school experiences. Journalist Walter Lippmann described stereotypes as "the pictures in our heads" that help people make predictions about what to expect from certain categories of people and draw conclusions about them even with incomplete information. The issue, as Aronson and Steele (2005) put it, is that while stereotypes "save us the trouble of thinking when we come into contact with people . . . they encourage simplistic thinking that ignores individual differences between people who belong to certain categories" (p. 438). In addition to the social implications of stereotyping, such overgeneralizations can have concrete impacts on student learning and performance. A multitude of studies have found that, regardless of how they are expressed, stereotyped ideas and expectations about intelligence can influence teacher treatment, impact academic performance, and influence how parents respond to children (Brophy & Good, 1974; Chang & Demyan, 2007; Dweck, 1999; Weinstein, 2002). As seen in Spencer's case, peers also can play a role in perpetuating stereotypes and shaping how students view their own intellectual ability (Aronson & Steele, 2005). In light of the threat that stereotypes impose, educational intervention models (such as Elliot Aronson's jigsaw method) have successfully attempted to foster a collaborative learning culture as opposed to a competitive one, reducing prejudice and promoting belonging (Aronson & Patnoe, 2011). Similarly, learning environments that support diversity rather than color-blindness also have been found to be effective at combating stereotype threat (Purdie-Vaughns & Eibach, 2008). Spencer himself noted similar qualities in Andrew's style of coaching and mentorship, encouraging teamwork, acceptance, and diversity. Andrew himself attributed these qualities to the activity itself, saying, "Debate produces a community which has to accept difference because you have to think about both sides and accept more than black and white. Even a kid who isn't popular or has a disability can win a debate round if they work hard enough."

DISIDENTIFICATION WITH SCHOOL

In the absence of strong adult mentors and cooperative support, Spencer, like many other students who fall victim to chronic failure (Griffin, 2002), responded by withdrawing emotionally from school, blaming teachers, claiming he did not care about doing well, and engaging in self-handicapping. As Aronson and Steele (2005) support, "Disidentification helps by reducing sensitivity to failure . . . but in the long-run, it hurts achievement because caring about doing well underlies the motivation for achievement" (p. 449). For Spencer, school was not only something he did not want to identify with, but something he viewed as running counter to his goals. He often would note that in school, the message was frequently that it was not okay to be patriotic, and that joining the military was an unacceptable future pathway. Instead, he often stated that his goal to join the Marine Corps stemmed from a desire "to make history." While he viewed school as a place where "you never learn anything you might actually use in the future," Spencer wanted to go into the Marines because "I want to make a difference." In the meantime, he pointed to modern-based warfare games as more aligned with his vision for the future. He recognized the existence of extreme gamers, but did not consider himself to be one—rather, he emphasized the power of video games to provide people with a second life, "a chance to imagine a life they might never have." During one of our visits to his home, Spencer elaborated on how video games help people express identities that otherwise might be constrained in the real world.

> SPENCER: In games you can definitely see the wide variety of different types of people. You really can. There are people who just come back from work, this is their rest. There's people who just come back from school, this is my rest. I hate school and this is how I take it out. And it shows people's creativity. Everything you can put in a game, it uses creativity.
>
> RESEARCHER: So it's like, to each his own?
>
> SPENCER: Yeah. You can be the person you want to be. It's surprising how different a person . . . I guess you can say this is kind of an example of how different a person is rather than the way they're stereotyped. 'Cause like you said, when most people think of me they think of like, swimming and games. People also think of me as patriotic American, Marines, all-out USA, but you'd also be surprised that I'm also a Soviet Union fan, which is one of the signs or emblems I can use in the game. I mean, there's more than you think behind the story. It really . . . like I said with creativity, it can bring out the person you never thought was actually there.
>
> RESEARCHER: And more than what you see on the surface?
>
> SPENCER: Yeah, definitely. The way you act in school is definitely going to be different than how you really are. And I guess, video games are a way to express who you actually are. You'd be surprised by the type of people you see on here. It's funny all the things you see that people put on there—smiley faces, hearts, sideways hearts, bursts, Soviet Union flags—and it's funny the stuff you see that people put up . . .
>
> RESEARCHER: Little pieces of identity.
>
> SPENCER: Yeah. It all depends on the person.

Although Spencer took solace in video games as an alternate universe to feel a sense of connection to the life he actually imagined for himself, in his real, everyday school life, the extent of his gaming activity often continued to feed negative stereotypes. Gaming was perceived as interfering with completing assignments, and his parents and teachers viewed it as a waste of time, reflecting the well-established discrepancy between adult and youth perspectives about digital media experiences (Herring, 2007). Many students would refer to him as "not wanting to learn," rolling their eyes and saying, "If practice makes perfect, then at least Spencer is perfect at video games." While his peers often chattered excitedly in huddled groups with him before class about their latest gaming sessions, when it came time for class to start, they would automatically open their books, raise their hands, and become students again. Only Spencer sat back and watched it all, rarely contributing to class discussions, which was odd for a former debater. To everyone else, this came as little surprise; based on his past behavior, no one expected him to.

HIDDEN CURRICULUM: RACE AND GENDER STEREOTYPES

While negative stereotypes can stem from assumptions based on past actions, they also can take hold even before any student behavior actually occurs. Many studies document gender discrepancies in school disciplinary actions and punishment from teachers (Coutinho, Oswald, & Best, 2002; Skiba, Michael, Nardo, & Peterson, 2002). Research points to an overrepresentation of boys in school disciplinary sanctions, and boys are over four times as likely as girls to be referred to the office or suspended (Cooley, 1995; Gregory, 1996; Imich, 1994). Boys are also significantly associated with the risk of being identified for special education services. For instance, a study by Coutinho, Oswald, and Best (2005) showed that, compared with White females, White males were 2.3 times more likely to be identified with a learning disability, and Black males were 5.5 times more likely to be identified with "serious emotional disturbance" (SED). Reports by the Indiana Education Policy Center and the American Association of University Women show that Black males are also more likely to be perceived less favorably by their teachers and tend to be referred to the office for less serious and more subjective reasons than White males.

Such discrepancies are further reinforced when White or Asian students are disproportionately placed in gifted and honors classes, teaching the "hidden curriculum" to students that some groups are inherently smarter (Noguera, 2003). This can happen as early as kindergarten, where Black boys are rated consistently lower by teachers for social behavior and academic expectations, and racial patterns begin to emerge with regard to tracking and ability grouping (Hilliard, 1991; Rong, 1996; Slaughter-Defoe & Richards, 1994; Tatum, 1997). Cultural messages and the mere knowledge of a stereotype can affect how students are treated, regardless of how a student actually behaves or performs in school (Steele, 1997). For Black males in particular, negative media images can impact how they are positioned in school, along with their access to important opportunities for learning (Davis, 2001; Meier, Stewart, & England, 1989). Unfortunately, studies show that "stereotype threat is strongest among students who are most invested in doing well, those who are highly identified with an intellectual domain" (Aronson & Steele, 2005, p. 449). Given the fragility of intellectual competence in the face of varying social relationships and perceptions, it is necessary to examine how students respond to the ways they are treated by others.

DEVIN: SMART AND BLACK

Devin Foster always thought of himself as a "smart" student, who was placed in the advanced track in middle school and was part of a group of friends whom everyone perceived as "successful." When he arrived home, his mother would greet him with an enthusiastic, "There's my college man!" and would describe him as "the one who is going to go places and put bread on the table." In fact, Devin joined debate primarily because it would help him get into college and prepare him for becoming a successful lawyer, and because it was "where smart kids go." He was naturally competitive and ambitious, and loved the challenge of coming up with strategies to prove his argument. At the end of the summer debate institute he attended before his first year of high school, he stated, "Thinking on your feet is hard. You have to be able to think quick to say something that's not too stupid to say." According to Devin, this type of intellectual activity was preferable to traditional classwork because "in school, you get credit for trying. In debate, you have to win." Although Devin had a difficult time with reading and writing, he rarely admitted to these struggles and often would say he received higher grades than he actually did in order to preserve his intellectual identity. His avoidance of his weaknesses made it difficult to actually address them, making him more vulnerable to the threat of stereotypes because of the high stakes of sustaining the "smart student" image (Aronson & Inzlicht, 2004).

Around his friends, Devin used the strategy of "racelessness" (Tatum, 1997) and rarely referred directly to being African American except to note to the team at the first tournament how few Black people were in debate. Instead, more of what he talked about was class differences between himself and his peers, along with the contrasts between his childhood in a primarily White suburb and his current situation in a high-poverty, urban center. He often would get nostalgic about the past abundance of extracurricular teams, which allowed him to take up softball at an early age. In contrast, his new neighborhood had fewer organized activities for teenagers, and it was important not to be viewed as academically oriented, because it would be seen in a negative and potentially dangerous light and invite charges of "acting White" (Fordham & Ogbu, 1986). At the same time, his mother, Ronda, refused to allow her sons to wear black-hooded sweatshirts—"hoodies"—because she did not want people to make assumptions about their intelligence. As a single mother of three whose husband had been shot when Devin was a child, Ronda was particularly protective of how people treated her children. Despite her objections, Devin occasionally would wear black hoodies to school and immediately noticed the difference in people's reactions.

> I used to come in with a black hoodie on, and they expect me to know no answers to the questions. Like the vice principal, he thought I was like a bad thing and he would look at me different . . . and then he found out, "Oh, you're in debate?!" and now he looks at me in a whole different way.

Both Devin and Ronda often would get annoyed at Black people who "gave other Black people a bad name." He noticed clear patterns in the classroom behavior in advanced classes with White and Asian students ("they all quiet in class") and in regular classes with largely Black and Hispanic students ("they all talkin' smart to the teacher and be acting like a fool in class"). Ronda often would get annoyed because this kind of behavior only continued to feed negative views toward Black students, especially in school.

> You see a Black kid come in and you just start expecting the worst. Even with my daughter, when I went to her class, I told her teacher that my daughter has some learning problems, but I do work hand and hand with her so if she's not doing something that you need her to do, call me and let me know. And she says to me, "I can see that already." And let me tell you why she says this, cuz my daughter, she's just very outgoing and really talkative and if you're around her you gonna see that. So my daughter went into the classroom and she friendly! She walked to the globe and started playing with it, and I guess that ticked her teacher off, cuz she says, "I can see she has some behavior problems because she walked in here and touched the globe. Most kids don't do that, most kids are shy when they come in." Well, my daughter is not shy! She's never been shy, never ever! So to expect her to come in shy and then put her in a category as a behavior problem child was wrong to me. Cuz you don't know her personality yet.

Devin had similar experiences with being treated differently in classes and having teachers assume the worst about him. During an observation in his 9th-grade science class, the first 30 minutes of the 90-minute block involved the teacher ignoring his complaints about not being able to see the board and not acknowledging his raised hand when she was directing questions to the whole class. During groupwork, however, as soon as she heard extra noise in Devin's direction (which actually came from a different group), the teacher immediately asked him to move across the room. The request was greeted with loud protests from Devin about having to move away from the computers that were required to complete the assignment, to which the teacher responded by writing him a referral to the office. Later on, Devin complained that she did not even write the correct name on the referral and could never remember his name when looking up his grades. In an interview with the teacher after the incident, she expressed shock that he was in debate because "he doesn't present himself as a serious student. He sits in the corner with friends and talks back to me. He is not very respectful and I send him out every other day."

Marginalization on the Debate Team

During his first year, Devin encountered similar situations in the debate class with Rebecca Miller, the same coach who previously had asked Anthony to leave the program. In an interview with her 2 months into the school year, Rebecca referred to Devin as "someone who distracts others from doing the work" and "who thinks of himself as a better debater than he actually is." He was frequently late turning in his speeches before tournaments and reading evidence packets, and often had to beg Rebecca to compete. In contrast, Devin would refer to himself as "a great debater," while his peers initially described him as "lazy" and "not willing to do the work." Regardless of which perspective was the most accurate, all of them intertwined to impact Devin's participation on the team. For instance, Rebecca's perception of Devin as "not willing to work" and her position of power allowed her to prevent his attendance at tournaments. Devin's perception, on the other hand, led to frustration with Rebecca as unreasonable and with other students as not helping him. His reading and writing difficulties also would compound the frustration, given the text-heavy nature of her assignments. Rebecca often found ways to call him out during class, rarely worked with him one-on-one, and isolated him from the group because she did not believe him to be "ready to participate." This type of marginalization was not unique to Devin but also extended to other members of the team (like Anthony), who did not meet Rebecca's expectations for quiet, focused behavior. She instead chose to work directly only with students who she felt "wanted to be there," an approach that created division within the team and tension toward her. Students eventually decided they wanted to attend tournaments regardless of their coach and resigned themselves to putting up with her decisions.

Devin's early experience on the debate team is only one example of the stigmatization of minority students. In schools that are White-dominant, racial minorities face a greater risk of peer rejection, social exclusion, and differential treatment by classmates (Baumeister & Leary,1995; Kistner, Metzler, Gatlin, & Risi, 1993). As a result, high-achieving middle and high school students can struggle academically due to increased awareness of social stereotypes (Aronson, Fried, & Good, 2002; McKown & Weinstein, 2003). Like Devin, students begin to notice patterns that show that Black students participate less frequently in rigorous activities such as debate, are on lists for suspension and remedial classes, and receive harsher punishments than other students (Ferguson, 2000; Oakes, 2005). At the same time, Noguera (2003) points out that "some Black students, including males, find ways to . . . manage to maintain their identities and achieve academically without being ostracized by their peers."

Transfer of Teacher Language to Students

The process of shifting the perceptions of his peers was complex for Devin. In particular, Katie, a student Rebecca identified as being "successful," often would use Rebecca's language to criticize students like Devin. During a session where Rebecca angrily left the room because students were not listening to her, Katie attempted a leadership role to defend Rebecca.

> KATIE: You guys, you know how rude that is right there. No matter how much of a jerk she can be sometimes, and I admit she can be a jerk, you are being so rude to her! (students protest, start to disagree with her)
> KATIE: Devin, please! Shut up! You guys are so disrespectful. Shut up and listen!
> STUDENT: Who made you the boss?
> KATIE: Guys! I'm going to do so bad at this tournament!
> (Devin reacts to student next to him)
> KATIE: Seriously, Devin, please! Are you serious? Why are you in debate in the first place? Cuz your counselor made you? Maybe you should transfer out! You're being immature . . . grow up! Half of you don't want to be in debate!

Although most students (even Katie) did not agree with Rebecca's philosophy or how she treated students, her discourse provided one of the only models for leadership in this setting. Phrases such as "why are you in debate in the first place?" or "maybe you should transfer out then!" were almost exact replicas of Rebecca's language toward students like Devin and continued the precedent that there were students whose participation could be restricted.

A Change in Positioning and Passing on Knowledge

While Rebecca's perception of Devin never changed, he was able to shift the perceptions of his teammates with the help of an intervention at his first overnight tournament. Upon arrival, Devin asked for my help in a panic, having not received assistance from Rebecca. Setting aside my role as a researcher (see Appendix), Devin and I worked together for an hour, where, as a former debater, I had him spontaneously explain arguments without text. I drilled him on the thesis of his arguments, clarified terminology, and drew diagrams to illustrate explanations. Devin was engaged in the strategy for connecting cross-examination to his rebuttals and, once he accepted that I did not want him to write anything down, immediately started practicing the techniques. He stopped the discussion, requesting to practice these techniques independently. As he paced back and forth, his teammates watched him practice statements about "value clash."

When he returned from his first round gushing about how well it had gone, his teammates initially did not believe him. While I did not intervene beyond the 1-hour interaction, he returned after every round with the same smile, saying to his peers, "It's all about the value clash. My opponent agreed that my criterion was the best way to achieve our goal of education, and I brought it back in the overview to my first rebuttal and extended it through the rest of the round." Katie was particularly intrigued and asked him about the new debate language he was using. He agreed to work with her, mirroring the language I had used. After staging a mock cross-examination session with her (which concluded with his statement, "I think you've got it now"), he was surrounded by the entire team asking him to coach them. The moment represented a shift in positioning for him, from novice debater to team mentor. Although he received several awards at that tournament, his actual record did not matter to the team, who already described Devin as "one of the better debaters." Katie bore no resentment toward Devin and instead exclaimed, "Did you see that? I was the one asking him questions!" She continued:

> It was really surprising he was actually teaching in a group and I was the one that was taking notes, which had never happened before. I really regret now what I had said during the class. Because now I realize what the others were talking about but, at the time, I didn't really see it. Like with how well Devin did, it really showed how well he worked with someone else [other than Rebecca]. I don't think most of us realized how much we didn't understand about our own cases.

While Rebecca left the team a few months later, Devin continued to ask for advice about how to learn to better teach others, a skill he continued to develop when I hired him as a teaching fellow for the following 3 years of the summer debate institute. He continued to participate on the debate team throughout his high school career, even when students like Katie left to pursue other activities. He had established his position as an integral part of the team.

RESISTING DISABLING PRACTICES

Both Spencer and Devin highlight the ways in which relationships with peers and teachers can directly impact a student's positioning and participation in and out of the classroom. Negative stereotypes and identity contingencies based on race, gender, and past behavior can limit people's perceptions about what they are capable of doing. Being positioned as "trouble" or "not wanting to learn" not only ignores the contextual influences on student participation but also restricts students' chances to develop the abilities necessary to remedy their situation (Harré & Moghaddam, 2003). The impact on student lives extends beyond a single moment in a classroom and also can result in "thickened," established identities developed around academic failure (Wortham, 2006). When the scope of what is possible for students is limited due to stereotyping, they lose access to opportunities that will help them pursue their goals, foster desired abilities, and expand control over their life trajectories. The extent to which their scope of possibility is restricted depends on their positioning as well as the perceptions of those with the power to exert influence.

Regardless of how constrained their participation might be, young people continue to push back on negative influences. For Devin, this meant his persistent involvement in a rigorous academic activity, proving his intelligence through intellectual competition, and challenging perceptions that Black men do not belong in debate. Spencer sought out modern-based warfare games to feel connected to his goals for the future of joining the Marines and took his GED to finally eliminate the obstacle of schooling. For both students, their efforts to drive the direction of their lives were influenced by a whole host of complex competing factors, including both negative perceptions from teachers and positive supports from them as well. Throughout their educational experience, both students had supportive resources that allowed them to exercise their agency and develop necessary abilities. Spencer, for example, was able to pursue his interests in debate and swimming with the help of coaches who promoted collaboration and positioned him as capable, and was unable to continue doing so after they left. The simple 1-hour coaching intervention on debate techniques provided Devin with the opportunity to shift the perceptions of his teammates and acquire the tools he needed to position himself differently on the team. Unlike Spencer, who was not close to anyone on the debate team, Devin also had a supportive network of peers, including those who initially had doubted his ability and a debate partner who helped sustain his involvement past the first year. Continued opportunities to teach others allowed Devin to maintain his status on the team and develop further as a debater. In this way, Devin's debate performance ability was framed as something that could always be improved (Dweck, 1999) and always carried the incentive of trophies, seals of distinction on his diploma, and proving himself to his peers. In Spencer's case, his academic history mandated that he always be viewed in a negative light by peers and adults, and that his performance and potential would remain static as long as he remained in the same school setting. He was afforded no opportunities to challenge these negative perceptions and improve his situation, particularly after he stopped receiving mentorship. Spencer was offered little recourse but to seek out other means of embarking on his own pathway, withdrawing himself from school entirely. Because the stakes are so high for students under threat of stereotypes, the influences on their scopes of possibility must be closely examined to discover strategies that might counter any harmful effects. According to Pedro Noguera (2003):

> Students can be unfairly victimized by the labeling and sorting processes that occur within school. . . . It is important to understand the factors that may enable them to resist these pressures and respond positively to various forms of assistance that may be provided within school or in the communities where they reside. (p. 442)

Contrary to beliefs about intelligence as an internal characteristic, the cases in this chapter reveal the intimate and far-reaching effects of social relationships on the student experience. Social inequities, persistent stereotypes, and assumptions about groups of people can threaten the development of abilities and the realization of personal goals. While it is often difficult to let go of the "pictures in our heads" and recognize the forces that play a role in creating them, doing so offers a chance to uncover students' true motivations, understand what they would like to be different, and encourage their ever-shifting identities.

Chapter 4

Images of Disability and Conflicting Identities

In two different high schools in two different states, James Ovill and Mark Browning sat at their desks, lined up in rows in science classes of 35 students each. James had his head down on the shiny surface, counting down the seconds until the bell rang. Mark had his hand raised, eager to be the first to answer the teacher's question about their latest lab. Despite the appearance that their behavior was solely a function of different levels of school motivation, for James and Mark, the driving force behind their actions lay past the initial picture of classroom participation. In addition to social relations and identity markers that shape the participation of all students (such as race, gender, and class differences), both of them were influenced by their personal relationship with their disability label. James, who deeply despised being labeled with Attention Deficit Hyperactivity Disorder (ADHD), often said he failed to see the point of science class, because he was never going to be a "good science student." Instead, he saw himself as a "scientist," an identity that he did not think could exist within the confines of academic expectations. And so he would put his head down in class, rarely sleeping, but instead waiting to leave the only place in his life where he was seen as "ADHD." Mark's identity, on the other hand, was dependent on performing well in school, as he desperately tried to prove to others that he could indeed sustain the identity of the "smart," "intellectual," and "slightly arrogant," successful student. He closely studied his classmates and sought behaviors that could help him distance himself from the label of autism, which he feared would lead people to think he was "cuckoo, crazy." He gave himself a different label of the "recovering autistic" and eagerly raised his hand to show he could do more than just "pass" for normal. He could be the best in the class.

While the previous chapter focused on stereotypes and the influence of social relationships on youth participation, this chapter examines how young people relate to their disability labels and how this relationship can influence their identities. The discussion necessarily revolves around how abilities are perceived by those around them and how those perceptions shape the ways they are positioned. Both cases involve 16-year-old Caucasian boys from middle-class families with well-educated parents, and explore the impact of negative messages about disability on the development of their academic identities. For both students, the self-perception that being labeled with a disability could act as a barrier preventing them from achieving their goals was reinforced by the impression that those who were not considered "successful" would not be treated favorably. Even just the underlying reality that they were being told they had a deficit related to academic performance implied a very real threat to their chances of developing desired abilities and a strong identification with academics. The cases illustrate different student responses to the pressure to become someone not associated with disability in order to achieve their goals and be viewed as "smart." By doing so, they elaborate on how the positioning dynamics in students' lives contribute to the construction of their identities and can be influencing factors in the possibility of pride in disability.

IDENTITIES IN MOTION

To revisit the definition described in the Introduction to this book, I define "academic identities" as personal perceptions of academic ability resulting from an ongoing process of self-understanding in relation to others, the demands of educational contexts, cultural definitions of academic success, and personal interests. How students think of their intelligence and potential to succeed is not tied solely to self-esteem, nor is it an individual opinion about oneself that can be viewed in isolation. Rather, how they identify with academic learning is a product of social relationships that are constantly in motion, "lived in and through activity" (Holland et al., 1998). Personal perceptions of ability continuously change with everyday experiences with other people and depending on what is required from the settings people encounter (Harré & VanLangenove, 1999; Holland et al., 1998; Raible & Nieto, 2008). What individuals care about and how their cares interact with the concerns of others drives the decisions they make, the experiences they seek, and the ways they participate, all of which can shape identity.

Social conditions and cultural norms continue to play a dynamic role in driving the process of how people take part in the world around them (Dreier, 2002; Holland et al., 1998). Throughout the complex, messy development of identities, the real work begins as people attempt to make sense of it all, respond to the contexts in which they live, and use their experiences to improvise possible selves and make choices about the future. As Michael Nakkula (2008) puts it, "Identity is the embodiment of self-understanding. We are who we understand ourselves to be, as that understanding is shaped and lived out in everyday experience" (p. 11). Academic identities are not a separate piece of this process, but instead, as Stanton Wortham (2006) theorizes, emerge jointly with social identification as people are positioned by others in terms of ability. For this reason, in school settings, adults wield incredible power over the academic identity development of their students through the ways in which they engage with and relate to students, and how they encourage (or discourage) students' relationship to academic learning (Nakkula, 2008). Nakkula and Ravitch (1998) describe this as a process of "reciprocal transformation," in which the most compelling positive influence on a young person's identity is when "it is clear to the student that she matters to the adult as much as the adult matters to her" (p. 20). Conversely, if students perceive that their efforts do not make a difference in the lives of others (particularly those who matter to them and can exert influence in their lives), they are less likely to be transformed by those experiences or develop lasting identities around them.

The Impulse to Categorize

There is an important tension between the notion that academic identities are always in flux over time and the creation of labels that restrict the expression of those identities. The disability labels and diagnoses themselves are not inherently the problem; rather, the problem is the tendency to assume that the labels can tell the whole story about a person. As Raible and Nieto (2008) describe in relation to the resurgence of race and ethnicity research in education, "We live in a time of transition, one in which static labels can no longer contain the rich complexity of contemporary identities" (p. 210). Similarly, just because a student is labeled with a disability does not mean that her needs, wants, goals, frustrations, interests, and successes remain static and unchanging. If anything, there is yet another layer of experience for which students must make meaning, working to understand for themselves what disability means for their life directions, opportunities, relationships, and any other matters that they deeply care about. Research in disability studies in education reveals that young people often are acutely aware of being surrounded by rigid attitudes about disability labels and social messages about the need to "fix" their disability (e.g., Kelly, 2005). Phrases in research literature that describe people with autism as "lacking a sense of self," "unable to participate in the construction of culture," or "individuals without a culture" are indicative of the disabling and discriminatory environments that young people often find themselves in (Baron-Cohen, 1993; McAdams, 1997). McDermott and Varenne (1996) call this mentality the "cultural deprivation approach," where people who are perceived as having "something wrong with them" are treated as inherently unable to be transformed through interaction and framed as the cause of their own failure (Vadeboncoeur & Portes, 2002). Instead, recent studies in fact show that students with autism do creatively craft identities and construct them through social relationships (Bagatell, 2003; Baines, 2012).

If disability is conceptualized as an aspect of human identity, rather than an individual impairment, then such messages are communicating to students that an aspect of who they are, is not acceptable. Such a mindset creates identity crises, instead of helping students resolve them, and poses the following dilemma: Either they do not identify with the part of their life that positions them in this way or they somehow must change who they are in order to be accepted. Young people face this dilemma whenever they encounter interactions that attempt to "hammer them into negative status positions," pigeonhole them into predefined categories, or put them into boxes "which specify the kinds of kids who do better than others" (McDermott et al., 2006, p. 15). Such interactions can come from anyone (teachers, parents, peers, to name a few), with important ramifications for how young people develop identities around academic learning.

JAMES IN THE GHILLIE SUIT

While James Ovill often appeared disengaged in class, upon closer examination he actually was doing a great deal of other work during class activities. An avid "nature man," he helped run an outdoor environmental education club at the school, which stemmed from his long-time interest in biology and the environment. During class, James often would be completing work on a nature trip he was organizing for a group of 50 students, arranging free transportation, getting district approval and creating permission forms, and planning a pretrip meeting for parents, where he would answer their questions. His father Charles noted the intense focus James could display from an early age whenever he was able to engage his passion for the environment, an interest that began with family camping trips and books on birds. Even when he was little, he would call himself a scientist and taught himself many of the survival techniques he used on nature trips. James lit up when discussing his experiences, particularly around one story of how he created a "Ghillie Suit," a type of camouflage clothing designed to look like heavy foliage. He spent hours on the suit, hand-weaving shredded fabric and leaves into copious amounts of fishnet until he could cover his entire body, staying up throughout the night until it was finished. James used the suit to fool his dad and brother in the backyard and also took it with him on the nature trips he organized.

Charles was rarely surprised by moments where James displayed intense focus, imagination, creativity, and an incredible sense of humor. James was the family comedian, creating skits, characters, and stand-up comedy acts to perform for friends and relatives. As time went on in school, what once was considered "funny" and "sociable" was viewed as "talking too much" or "not being able to sit still." James felt like he often disappointed his teachers, who expected more from the younger sibling of an academically successful older brother, and that his personal projects allowed him to take pride in the fact that he "could do something." From 1st grade, James had to face the startling difference between his actively engaged scientific pursuits at home and the stressful or boring science classes at school. For Charles, the entire process of James's getting diagnosed with a disability was somewhat confusing and begged the question of what was so different about the school context, rather than what was wrong with James.

> We've had James tested to a degree by psychologists and everyone agrees that he's very smart . . . very personable, very articulate . . . he has a bit of ADHD, and a question I certainly have is, is that amount of ADHD . . . is that a bug or a design feature? Take James out of that school setting and he's a leader. On these trips, he's the one who is scouting things out, who is keeping the group together, who is encouraging all of the other kids, he's the one who builds an igloo so he and his buddies can sleep warm and gets up the next morning and makes hot drinks for the other kids who are shivering in wet tents.

As both James and Charles pointed out, even in elementary school, there was little opportunity for James to display the dimensions of identity that he was known for outside of school, such as "the nature man" or "the comedian." Being labeled with ADHD solidified his reputation as someone who could not focus and who could not seem to master school-sponsored methods of learning. He instead continued his nature learning via countless hours of Internet research, books, science shows on television, and outdoor experiences with his family and friends.

James at School: "We Already Know What Is Going to Happen"

By the time he reached high school, James viewed academics as something he just needed to "get through" and did not personally identify himself as a "good student." He did not come to such a conclusion lightly and, like many other students, would approach the beginning of every school year with renewed enthusiasm and optimism that something would be different. Unfortunately, he could identify countless experiences in school where he felt like he did not belong or that his abilities were not appreciated or valued, especially once he was diagnosed with ADHD. These experiences were traumatic at first, such as in 1st grade when he would come home and sob about work he could not do, saying, "I won't be forgiven." As time progressed, he became comfortable with the conflict between his image of himself as intelligent and his poor academic performance by reasoning that school had no means of actually appreciating his skills.

> RESEARCHER: Do you think of yourself as a smart person?
>
> JAMES: Yeah, but I don't think the school does.
>
> RESEARCHER: Oh really? Say more about that.
>
> JAMES: Well, I don't know, the last 2 years I really didn't do well in school. Um, I don't really know what to say except that I really didn't do a lot of my work, even though I knew how to do it. This year it's better though, I just like, over the summer of sophomore year, I heard you get a lot more mature or whatever, so I guess that happened.
>
> RESEARCHER: When do you feel like the school treats you as someone who's not smart?
>
> JAMES: Um, I guess it's like, they only really look at your grades, it's not like there's any other measurement system other than test scores. Um, I've always taken longer on tests because I think about it a lot, so, I just don't think they have a good way of telling intelligences and then getting into colleges . . . they definitely don't know anything about you.
>
> RESEARCHER: So it's like, you don't think schools are able to get a real picture of what the kid is capable of.
>
> JAMES: Yeah, and like, maybe an individual teacher will, but it's not going to show anywhere that matters.

Interviews with Charles focused on more specific problems James had in school, such as struggles he had with math, getting work in on time, or talking too much in class. "He's not a slouch," Charles pointed out. "Meeting the requirements set in school is really tough for him, but he knows a lot." On a broader level, James was much more attuned to the institution of school itself and why he did not identify with its central definitions of learning and success. While he rarely acted out in class, James often would withdraw when he felt that the culture of the school and its classrooms was too rigid and wished that he had the freedom to explore and set the parameters of his own learning. He was extremely suspicious of the purpose behind most assignments, as well as work that did not feel authentic.

> I do not like busy work one bit. I feel like for me, just the teaching process itself is inefficient really. A teacher can lecture about something for 2 hours and you have to listen the whole time and it's not very interesting because it's just a voice and you have to retain all this stuff. As a kid, I

used to love watching NOVA and all these things on Channel 9 and I learn so much better from watching a show, like I can remember everything from watching a show.

For James, school was not a place where he could transform himself and others, expand his scope of possibilities, or develop abilities related to helping him control the direction of his life. He pointed to the absence of control over learning as part of why he would lose motivation throughout the year. His lack of interest in the activities required to get a good grade "just kind of accumulates and I don't really want to do it anymore and I lose motivation." This perception and self-understanding made it difficult for him to identify with school and academic learning, particularly when (as we would see later in our home visit) his own goals, interests, and way of learning were so much in contrast with the demands of the school and definitions of academic success.

James's high school, Jefferson High, was not unusually rigid in its structure, and in fact took steps to address the issue of academic relevance that James often complained about. At roughly 1,600 students, consistently high test scores, and 23 students to every teacher, the numerical picture showed Jefferson to be, at the very least, a traditional American high school that arguably could offer a better academic experience than most. We selected Jefferson because of its partnership efforts with a local university to make science more relevant for students (particularly those in college prep or lower track classes). The program entailed having a graduate student in the natural sciences come in to the regular classes weekly to work with students on various labs and speak to them about work as a scientist. In James's case, this opportunity also happened to be combined with the implementation of a curriculum effort to help students develop action research projects related to their communities and home lives. Despite clear attempts from the school and science teacher, these efforts were not enough for James to feel a connection with school, as he still perceived the activities as not authentic and the interactions as not positioning the students as experts. "It's pretty cool that Alex comes into class," James recognized. "But I dunno . . . he seems like he's kind of, treating us kinda younger, I guess. The class is mixed skill levels, so maybe that's necessary. But some of the stuff he does is oversimplified . . . or I've heard it before . . . or it doesn't go in depth."

Over the course of the semester, observations of the class revealed students to be mostly silent in groupwork; discussions took place with four active student volunteers, who did not include James. According to the teacher, Ms. Simms, the biggest issue in the class was attendance and turning in the required assignments. James often was paired with Anderson, a student labeled with autism who was one of the few who constantly raised his hand in class. In labs, Anderson often spoke quickly and authoritatively, taking copious notes, while James moved through the procedures slowly with a bored expression before putting his head down on the desk with his eyes closed. In one particular lab, James was working with Anderson and another student on a question of competition between plants, by planting grasses and radishes in different levels of densities with or without fertilizer. While labs often would peak James's attention, he closed his eyes immediately after the graduate student Alex stated, "What I'm going to do here is actually tell you what our methods are going to be with this experiment." The following discussion took place later on in the class period:

> ANDERSON: Alright group, I have it all planned out. So what are we doing, I know what we're doing, but what group are we . . . are we the fertilizer group?
>
> JAMES: We're the fertilizer group, grass, high density.
>
> ANDERSON: Okay, so how many pots do we need to get?
>
> JAMES: I think we get six pots. (talks to another student who walks by, inaudibly, then to Anderson while looking at an explanation on the board) So we're grass, six pots, with fertilizer, for 40 seeds . . . I think that's per pot. (pause) This isn't much of an experiment. It's like we already know what's going to happen.
>
> ANDERSON: (silently writing, away from James) So, all the cups are fertilized?
>
> JAMES: Yeah.
>
> ANDERSON: (scribbles furiously in his notebook, calculating numbers out loud to figure out how many seeds go in each pot, based on the area. James watches and Lee, their third group member, walks over to join them for the first time. The number Anderson comes up is exactly the one written on the board)
>
> ANDERSON: I thought we were supposed to figure this out. I'm confused. Why would they make us do this? It's like they're telling us exactly what to do.
>
> JAMES: They always do.
>
> ANDERSON: (pauses, staring at the board) So, we're supposed to add . . . but we have six cups, not three cups.
>
> JAMES: So, yeah, it's 40 grass seeds in each of the six pots, I'm guessing, because of the slash, I guess that means per pot.
>
> ANDERSON: So which one do we measure, if it's all the same?
>
> JAMES: (yawns and stretches) It depends on what (air quotes) "we decide." (gets up to get materials)

Despite Anderson's initial enthusiasm, the prescribed nature of the lab activity allowed James to confirm and pass on the same cynical message he had already subscribed to: School learning did not constitute real-world learning. His mockery of school attempts to grant students power over their own learning (signified by the air quotes) and bored recognition that they were discovering something that had already been discovered, shed a new light on the role that context played in his ADHD diagnosis. School officials had identified him as lacking focus, hyper, and easily distracted, but given the nature of his identification with academic learning, this kind of behavior would not be surprising. The image of school as disconnected from real-life learning and the perception of himself as "not a good student" persisted even when James was given the opportunity to do an action research project that directly connected to his life. As James put it:

> I was kind of interested in that because it was a real thing for once, but um, it ended up being the reason I didn't do well that semester. I was just tired from all of the other stuff. I did part of it but then it was kind of big and not really . . . I dunno. I feel Ms. Simms tries to bring in assignments that aren't that structured and I usually would want to do that. But in that setting it just seems kind of weird because most of the kids there don't like that kind of thing. So she always just seems defeated by the class and it's hard to take some of that stuff seriously.

For James, it was not enough to implement a single intervention or program when it did not also address his personal history and identity around school or the fundamental contextual arrangement of classroom dynamics. Regardless of the activity, the attitudes and concerns of the people around him, culture of the classroom, and how students were being positioned by teachers governed whether learning could be viewed as meaningful. James's perception that Alex would oversimplify material, or the fact that students were told explicitly how to do the lab, ensured that no matter what they were asked to do, the traditional structure of schooling would remain the same. While this meant that the interventions could not address James's complaints about a lack of connectedness to school, they also did not alleviate the core issues he had with schooling and the academic identity he had built around it. Even when he was given freedom to connect learning to his everyday life, he still did not have the tools to combat the image, established over many years in the educational system, of being "ADD" or "not a good student."

James's case revealed once again how students have a tendency to gravitate to where they feel like they can make a difference, transform others and themselves, and be appreciated by those who can exert control in their lives. The nature trips allowed him to exercise his agency and develop the abilities that he viewed as essential to achieving his goals in life. While his teachers were not aware of James's reputation as the nature guy, his peers recognized his position as the group leader and looked to him for guidance in precarious outdoor situations. James was aware of the contrasts between his in-school and out-of-school identities, particularly around his ability to focus and pay attention in his learning experiences. He was able to resolve these contradictions by caring less about establishing a "good student" identity, which he believed had little role to play in his future goal of becoming an environmentalist. Nature trips represented authentic and meaningful learning for James, allowing him to position himself as a leader and have a sense of power that he did not have in school.

POSITIONING AND DISABILITY

Understanding the ways in which students position themselves and are positioned by others in school "offers a way to identify and disrupt deficit identities as they are being formed" (Collins, 2013, p. 14). In the face of ability measures that sort them according to rates of learning, students are categorized in ways that can be difficult to escape unless there are concentrated efforts to disrupt such "systematically haphazard" patterns (McDermott et al., 2006). The difficulty is that youth identities often are treated as a side effect of academic experiences or a hobby that students should set aside in order to finish their work, rather than the self-perceptions and understandings that actively influence all learning. How students perceive themselves and interpret who they are in relation to those around them is at the core of what drives their actions, choices, and participation. As Nakkula (2008) describes, the development of identities is an ongoing process of "integrating successes, failures, routines, habits, rituals, novelties, thrills, threats, violations, gratifications, and frustrations into a coherent and evolving interpretation of who we are" (p. 11). Positioning moments can form patterns that allow identities to "thicken" and strengthen over time, and allow others to identify an individual as a "certain type of person" or as "disabled" (Collins, 2013; Holland & Lave, 2001; Wortham, 2006). When certain opportunities for ability development are associated with certain types of students, students who do not fit that image are restricted from participating and therefore are prevented from developing particular dimensions of the identities they wish for themselves.

How students respond to these social restrictions often depends on whether students view their disability as interfering with their personal goals. Dreier (2009) argues that personal change often can begin when people face tensions and contradictions that get in the way of the lives they wish to lead or when people pursue ways to improve their life conditions. This personal change occurs amid what Harré and Moghaddam (2003) call "webs of storylines," which describe the events, histories, and cultural practices that contextualize people's actions. Positioning theorists argue that examining storylines helps clarify how events unfold following already established patterns of development and form patterns of actions that are recognized and used to categorize behavior (Harré, 2008; Harré & Moghaddam, 2003; Slocum & Van Langenhove, 2003). Storylines of ability communicated to students throughout their academic histories are revealed in the patterns of how students are treated by others in school. Understanding how individual students are situated within these patterns highlights what motivates their behavior. Rather than being restricted by the same storylines that consistently position them as "disabled," Sadowski (2008) argues that "students need the freedom to explore their unfolding identities and form new identifications based not on outmoded, confining labels, but on their real needs" (p. 222).

MARK: "I USED TO BE AUTISTIC, BUT NOT ANYMORE"

While both boys represent cases of students whose personal images and goals conflict with their disability labels, James responded by distancing himself from school, and Mark Browning responded by trying to change himself to better fit academic expectations. Throughout his experiences in school, Mark viewed himself as "smart" and took pride in his mastery of historical events and political expertise. In history class, he was the person that other students turned to when they wanted to know the answer, the one they would copy from, and the one who teachers would call on in class discussions. Even in elementary school, a 6-year-old Mark wrote a story for the class entitled "Why I Love My Atlas." To maintain his desired level of knowledge, he established a practice of printing, reading, and filing the latest world news each day, which helped him not only in class assignments but also in debate rounds.

Mark's vision of himself as an advanced student regularly contrasted with his being diagnosed with autism at age 2. He received special education supports all the way through elementary school, but experienced an identity shift in 8th grade, when he decided that he did not belong in a special education class with students with more visible, physical disabilities. His mother, Kathy, believed this might have been because he did not view himself as belonging to that particular category and asked himself, "I can see why she needs to be in here because she's disabled physically, but why am I in this class?" By the time he got to high school, Mark began describing himself as "recovered, or cured . . . or past that. I *was*, I *had* autism when I was younger." He distanced himself from the special education class with Ms. Hayes (who was also Anthony's teacher) because he did not want to be associated with having a disability any longer, although he still had an IEP through his senior year and had the option of going to the resource room for help.

RESEARCHER: Now, talk about Ms. Hayes's class a little, do you have her class now?

MARK: Uh, no. I used to have her class back in middle school, and that was sort of a special ed class, cuz I'm sort of a little bit autistic in a way, but not really, so basically in high school, she would let me off the leash and let me do stuff, but she checks on me every once and a while. She goes and asks people how I'm doing and stuff like that, you know.

RESEARCHER: What do you mean by "autistic in a way, but not really"?

MARK: When I was 2, I couldn't really talk. And so, my parents were really worried that I was going to become really autistic and stuff, but then, you know . . . thanks to a lot of circumstances that sort of really helped me and I sort of overcame my autism.

According to Ms. Hayes, Mark would say that being labeled as autistic was "unacceptable." Instead, he wanted to be viewed as "smart," "intellectual," and "the best in the class." Unlike James, he was desperate to be on his "best behavior" in school, which he defined based on what others expected of "smart students." He often would speak about managing the perceptions of other people to maintain his identity, saying, "I'm always thinking about controlling people's impressions. I'm always, like, thinking about what do I really want to do in this school, I'm always like, strategizing like, what do I really want to show people at times, you know?" Mark would describe this process as something he could manage personally, because "it's up in here (gesturing to head) what I decide I want to do." Mark continued, "I just sort of, uh, switch to and fro . . . it's sort of like what do you wanna be during the day, sort of like that." Mark's efforts to be seen as smart extended to choices about activities, goals, friends, and actions in the classroom. To be considered "smart," he observed and identified the following requirements for best behavior: He needed to get As, turn in his work, finish on time, listen to the teacher, raise his hand and participate in discussions, follow directions, remember facts, and know the correct answers. He followed all of these requirements and maintained a 4.0 GPA throughout high school, enrolling in the most challenging AP classes. He avoided the resource room and special education teachers or aides, and joined the debate team, where the "intellectual students" were.

SUPPORTING AN ACADEMIC IDENTITY

Mark's quest to be viewed as intellectual began at an early age, even before he relabeled himself as a recovered autistic. His special education teacher,

Ms. Hayes, worked with him from 1st grade all through high school, and remembered how in elementary school he always wanted to be first in line to go into the classroom. In reaction to several difficult situations where Mark would push other students in order to be first, she would use colors to help him express his feelings, and pictures and stick figures to illustrate how, no matter what place he was in line, he would always make it through the door. As he got older, they practiced setting goals and stating reasons behind those goals, and would play games set up so he did not win, in order to help him cope with disappointment. In high school, Ms. Hayes noticed that Mark was a great deal more flexible, but still had a hard time "losing," such as when he yelled at a teacher after not getting an A on a paper, or when he got angry in PE if the other team scored too many points with him as goalie. In those "teaching moments," Ms. Hayes acted as a "no excuses" facilitator, communicating with teachers, letting them know about the behavior they might see, and helping them set boundaries and diffuse difficult situations using concrete, visual tools.

People who spent time with Mark either deeply appreciated the extent of his efforts or did not even notice any fundamental differences. His peers on the debate team occasionally would describe him as eccentric and "following his own rules," but also would identify him as the "hardest working member of the team." They recognized his dedication to the team with the "Legacy Award," given to the student who contributed the most to ensuring the future of the team. His parents credited his membership on the debate team with providing him with the clear participation structures, speaking skills, and opportunities for team collaboration that supported his efforts to interact with others. Similarly, Ms. Hayes noted that "it helps that Hillside has been so supportive and everyone knows him. He understands the structure, the routine." Mark's family admired and encouraged his expertise in history and politics, by taking trips to historical sites to connect what he was learning in books to actual places in the real world. His teachers valued his expertise, and the physics teacher, Mr. Steffani, characterized Mark as having "intellectual power filtered through some unusual behavior" as ultimately admired by other students. Mr. Steffani noted:

> He can reel himself back in extremely quickly and make little corrections once he gets a little guidance to see the big picture. To perceive his mistakes and the context of those mistakes and how to fix them is pretty impressive and happens so quickly . . . he exercises a lot of control. This is hard for a lot of students and makes me wonder, to what extent does the label determine the outcome? If students were to unlabel themselves, what would happen?

Threats to the "Smart" Identity

In contrast to his "best behavior," Mark referred to moments that threatened his academic identity as "slips," where he would worry about what others would think of him and whether they would ever respect him again. "Slips" ranged from occasions when he would yell at a teacher, push another student, or exhibit behavior associated with autism (e.g., jumping or handflapping), or even times when he did not perform as well as others. At one debate tournament in particular, Mark did well but not as well as Katie (the 1st-year student who had transformed her opinion of Devin in the previous chapter). The fact that he, as a junior and veteran debater, had been beaten by a younger student angered Mark deeply, even though he also had performed well.

> RESEARCHER: You don't have to compete with your team—there isn't a point.
> MARK: Yes there is . . . otherwise, they won't respect me! They won't clap for me!

For Mark, individual performance was not enough to prove that he was intelligent. Instead, individual performance was always viewed in comparison with other students, and he feared that people would begin to see him as unsuccessful. As a debater, Mark worked hard to control any autistic "slips" and was able to compete against other students at an advanced level at state and national tournaments without judges noticing that he was any different. The activity itself meant a great deal to Mark, as winning debate rounds represented the ultimate academic achievement and primary means of proving to others that he was smart.

> MARK: When you're trying to get As, it doesn't really matter what you say, you can say anything you want and if it looks good, the teacher will give you an A, but in debate, you can't just do that, cuz if you say something really stupid, then the opponent can turn it on you and you lose.
> RESEARCHER: Do you think that's better than having As?
> MARK: Well . . . I don't know, like, while getting good grades, it makes me feel proud, but it doesn't really do anything, but winning debate rounds . . . it just makes me so happy. Just conquering my enemies.

In order to conquer his enemies, Mark believed that he could not also be associated with the label of autism. Despite efforts by his family and Ms.

Hayes to reinforce the unique, positive elements of his disability, Mark's perception of autism (as shaped by societal messages about the disability) was that a person could not be simultaneously disabled and smart. In his special education exit meeting during senior year, he was adamant that colleges not know about his disability, either on his applications or when he began classes. "I don't want them to see me as someone who needs help all the time!" Mark shouted. "They absolutely cannot know I used to be . . . you know, cuckoo, crazy! I'm not crazy!" His determination to maintain a strong academic identity in the eyes of others extended to his behaviors at home as well. Whenever he returned home from school, he would shut the door to the den, put on military marching band music, and spend 10 to 15 minutes jumping and flapping his arms, which his close friend Gaby called "The Snoopy Dance." This behavior was compartmentalized and restricted to that window of time, after which he would never act in any way that could be interpreted by others as "autistic." Similar to findings by linguistic anthropologist Shirley Brice Heath, Mark wanted to think of himself "as a who and not a what" (Heath & McLaughlin, 1993). He wanted to be seen in the eyes of others as successful in his own right and not according to assumptions about autism.

The Pressure to "Not Be Different"

Despite efforts to help him deal with disappointment and failure, Mark experienced intense anxiety around the need to maintain a strong academic identity. The stakes were high—he believed that any single incident could cost him his reputation as successful, threaten his friendships, and limit his opportunities. While he enjoyed and benefited from debate tournaments socially and academically, not every student shared his anxieties, which was particularly frustrating to Mark when he felt that he cared more about his losses than his debate partner or teammates did. Defining himself as "the best" also had the natural consequence of treating others as less worthy than him, particularly around race and class. In statistics class, for instance, he occasionally would make generalizations about Black people having lower rates of success in life because they were poor, much to the dismay of many of his classmates. Such comments were made less in regard to inherent racism and more in connection to the ingrained message that difference from the norm was not acceptable if one wanted to succeed.

The high-stakes pressure he felt in always having to define and protect himself in comparison with others contrasts with the more traditional myth of the autistic person as being alone and isolated from sociocultural dynamics (Biklen, 2005). According to Aurora, one of the other researchers, "Everyone assumes kids with autism don't realize what's going on. Society puts pressure on them to learn how to adapt to their environments, so that they aren't perceived as different. That's what a lot of high school is about—for all kids, but kids with autism, too." Although Mark learned to adapt to situations with others and worked to position himself as smart, he still had to resolve the contradiction he perceived between success and disability. He saw no other choice but to disassociate himself from the label that would interfere with how others viewed his abilities. After graduation, he went on to a 4-year college and was accepted into several internships in politics, all the while keeping his promise not to mention his disability to anyone. His motives around maintaining a strong academic identity were clear—but what was sacrificed in the process of fitting into preconceived notions about smartness?

STUDENT RELATIONSHIPS WITH DISABILITY LABELS

Although James and Mark responded to their disability labels in completely different ways, they both were driven by the desire to develop and sustain the identities, self-images, and pathways that mattered most to them. They took great pains to position themselves in ways that gave them power over the perceptions of others and to expand what was possible in their lives. This positioning took place directly in relation to their personal goals and visions of the future. In Mark's case, his goal to be academically successful meant that he had to deeply engage in school in order to position himself as "the best." James instead distanced himself from the school setting because that was the only place he was viewed as "ADHD." His goals were supported and fulfilled outside of school, where he could position himself as a leader.

In both cases, the students were inundated with storylines and images of the ideal, successful student that forced them to choose whether to adapt and change themselves or disregard academic ideals and pursue their own course. Their actions were driven by the need to resolve contradictions between societal perceptions and how they viewed themselves, in ways that made the most sense in their lives. How they positioned themselves contributed directly to the development of their identities, which in their cases meant that disability was viewed as something to be distanced from. Pride in their disabilities might have been possible had the labels not been perceived by the students as interfering with their goals or resulting in negative perceptions from others. Instead, James and Mark illustrate how young people want to feel like they can transform their worlds, challenge the perception of helplessness, and play a role in the development of their own identities, on their own terms.

SUMMARY: PATTERNS OF YOUTH RESISTANCE

James Ovill and Mark Browning represent two ways that young people can navigate negative positioning and resist external forces that restrict their freedom to pursue what matters most to them. The six case studies presented so far illustrate how young people respond to disabling and stigmatizing treatment in ways that reassert the identities they imagine for themselves. Their acts of resistance are related to the development of abilities that allow them to exercise agency and take an active part in shaping their lives and future goals. While their stories by no means encompass all possible forms of resistance, they represent three patterns that interpret youth responses in terms of agentic action, rather than dismissing them as classroom disruption, lack of motivation, or laziness. Based on common themes across their responses, the cases in Parts I and II of this book can viewed in summation as "challengers," "creators," and "rebels." Each kind of response is in relation to a specific set of external forces, and resistance takes on a different form depending on the individual's motives, self-perceptions, and future goals. Table 4.1 summarizes the three patterns across the different case studies.

Although Table 4.1 describes different forms of youth resistance and identifies specific connections to ability development and future goals, it is not enough simply to be aware of the responses to disabling practices. If young people are left alone in their efforts, and their resistance is not supported or facilitated by those around them, several problems can arise. Table 4.2 outlines the issues students can encounter and suggests possible approaches that directly address youth responses to disabling practices and shift perceptions away from simplistic assumptions about their identities.

The patterns synthesized in the two tables consider ways in which young people react to shifts in how they are positioned and how they push back in order to develop abilities in service of their future goals, which relates to the "ability as agency" framework. Rather than reacting to the outward behavior, the suggestions listed here work to uncover some of the social dynamics and personal identity issues underlying resistance. Since actions and personal change often are driven by a desire to make sense of the contradictory elements of life, it is important to examine the source of any contradictions. For challengers like Mark and Devin, resistance efforts are necessary to resolve conflicts between how they perceive their own intelligence and how others view them as a result of social stereotypes. As creators, Tinsley and James worked hard to manage contradictions between their personal goals and school values by blending in or disengaging from class environments and creating a whole separate world to develop important abilities. Anthony and Spencer might have been positioned as troublemakers in school, but their re-

TABLE 4.1. Three Forms of Youth Resistance

Form of Resistance	Cases	Reasons Behind Response	External Forces to Resist	Relation to Developing Abilities	Relation to Future Goals
Challenger	Mark, Devin	Desire to prove they are smart (join debate team, get good grades, win competitions, have the smartest friends)	Societal stereotypes related to race and disability, positioned as unsuccessful by teachers or peers, negative perceptions of ability by others	Develop academic skills (e.g., public speaking) and master academic material	Attending 4-year, top-tier university and go into financially secure profession, like law or politics
Creator	James, Tinsley	Blend in at school, stay under the radar, and create a completely separate space to pursue passions and develop skills	Talents unrecognized in school, academic material not connected to interests, stressful school histories, restricted participation in unsafe learning spaces	Develop and practice abilities related to personal interests and goals (e.g., nature trips, novel writing)	Achieving long-time career goals, like becoming a writer or a scientist
Rebel	Anthony, Spencer	Defiant rejection of school as irrelevant to goals, sabotage own performance to protect and position self in front of others, keep true passions private	Positioned as unsuccessful, disruptive, or unmotivated; limited opportunities to display strengths and develop abilities; tense interactions with educators	Pursue career trajectory separate from school and not dependent on school success, seek out established alternative pathways	Achieving long-time career goals, such as entering the military

TABLE 4.2. Supporting Youth Resistance

Youth Response	Problem If Left Unsupported	Shift in Approach
Challenger	To prove they are smart, students sometimes have to deny a part of who they are, have to ignore their weaknesses, and can be unprepared for failure or face an identity crisis if they do not succeed.	Appreciate that they perceive themselves as smart and help them in fulfilling this identity while also supporting them in discovering and addressing areas of need. Do not try to beat them down or prove they can never maintain a "smart student" image.
Creator	Since they do not perceive school as a safe place to pursue passions (and often find it boring), their ability development and identities can be threatened if they lose access to outside opportunities to pursue what they love.	Understand how and where they learn, analyze what captures their interest and what they need in order to feel safe in school, and make sure learning experiences are active with clear purpose and real-world applications. Do not assume they are passive or goalless.
Rebel	In the process of rejecting school expectations, students can feel victimized or like they do not belong, reinforcing the idea that they also must reject school-related support and sabotage their performance to stay in control.	Research personal histories behind negative relationship with school, pay attention to how language is used toward them, be a good listener, be unpredictable but fair, and create authentic challenges. Do not react solely to surface behavior, patronize or blame them for failure, or assume they are lazy or unmotivated.

sistance was characterized by attempts to position themselves as leaders who could make a difference in the world, regain control over their lives, and pursue alternative pathways. Despite their complex efforts, young people cannot be entirely responsible for resolving conflicts in their lives, developing the abilities they will need to expand the scope of possibilities available to them, or pushing back against disabling practices. Recognizing and valuing their efforts is the first step in disrupting deficit identities as they are being formed. Many social dynamics come into play when negatively positioning youth; in turn, a whole host of influencing factors are needed to help reposition them as capable, valued citizens.

Part III

THE POWER TO REPOSITION YOUTH

To be appreciated by others, it takes understanding and you gotta want to listen to somebody, give them a chance . . . and you need honesty, not only to other people, but honesty to yourself, because if you're able to show your true side to people then they can trust you more. And sometimes, you just gotta be the one to do something, jump in and try it out, that's part of what life is, jumping in blind. You need both the opportunity to grow and you need the courage to go out into the world and be yourself.

—Colby Simpson, 15

Impromptu

The self-proclaimed debate water boy was persistent, standing in the doorway of Room B308 before each debate class. With his large frame and courteous greetings, he reminded me of a bouncer in a fancy club or a restaurant host, guarding the entrance to the activities inside but never invited in. It wasn't until the team hired a coach to teach an additional event called "impromptu speaking" that Anthony found his entrance once again.

It was a model of speaking that would have terrified me as a high school student. With no resources and only 2 minutes to prepare a 5-minute speech on a random word, quote, or current event, it rewarded the masters of random information. Impromptu speakers were charismatic, humorous, and spontaneous, and the event often appealed to students who hated the research and writing aspect of other events. For Anthony, he loved that he would be able to talk about whatever he wanted without being constrained by additional rules. He had found his place. He was finally allowed to be the stand-up comedian of the debate class. He could incorporate points about the military into every speech and people had to listen. While at the beginning of the year he attended the first Lincoln–Douglas debate tournament dressed in his nicest suit, he had chosen not to actually compete. With impromptu, he never hesitated before signing up.

At 7:00 in the morning at the subway station, the members of the Hillside debate team huddled together in a tight, sleepy circle, dressed in suits with sweatshirts thrown over them. The crisp, chilly air was almost enough to ward off the drowsiness of the morning, especially when combined with nerves and, for Anthony, two Rockstar Monster energy drinks. As we waited for two students who were almost always late, Anthony joked with the others, showing not a shred of apprehension about the day to come.

We arrived at the school and directed Anthony to his assigned classroom. In the room, he looked around with inquisitive eyes and seemed amused by the scared facial expressions of his young opponents. He was fifth speaker, so he sat and watched the other students with a smirk on his face and his chin on his hand. When he received his topic, he looked it over but didn't write anything down or use any preparation. He walked up confidently and smiled at the audience.

"Today, I'm going to talk to you about tradition, like the 420 tradition . . . hold close what America holds great! Hehe . . . personally, my family is Swiss and we have a lot of traditions. Um, I'm trying to think. Football, there's a lot of tradition in that but personally, I just like watching because of the cheerleaders. Palestine and Israel have a lot of traditions but that gets them into trouble a lot of the time. Um, civil rights, the stripes on the flag . . . tradition always represents something. IHOP, that's one of my favorite traditions. Mmmm . . . hashbrowns, they're delicious! I mean, what are your guy's traditions? Anybody, anybody? And yah, thank you very much."

His judge and opponents looked a little shocked by his speech, and Anthony looked over at us with a helpless expression on his face, sticking out his lower lip. As we all exited the room, Anthony said to us loudly, "Oh god, I totally lost." The judge smiled at him and patted him on the back. He was silent on his way back to the cafeteria, but once he saw his classmates, he rushed over to the table and immediately joined in on the group's collective venting session about the first round. "I just got up there and started BSing, you could tell the judge was a liberal so I tried to talk about things he would like. And I was all like, UMMMMM . . . and just started filling up time and talked about football and hashbrowns. It had to be fun, I just can't do a speech that isn't just me goofing off for 5 minutes. That's what I rely on is just BSing, it's what I do. I'm going to be a novice forever so what do I care?" As we walked to his second round, he privately turned to us and said, "Did you see me talking to the team? I was all calm and composed before with the judge and stuff. But when I get back with my teammates I act totally crazy. And I act more autistic." The rest of the day went similarly to the first round, and as it wore on, he almost looked forward to the venting sessions with his teammates after rounds. He did not reserve his presence only for the Hillside team but sat down with students from other schools, blending into their conversations. Wherever he sat, he looked like a member of their team, and explosions of laughter would erupt from different corners of the room, depending on where he was telling his latest story. "He's like our very own debate ambassador!" exclaimed one Hillside student, with a somewhat wistful tone in her voice. "Only Anthony could go and talk to all those people we don't even know!" By 3:00 that afternoon, the final round was posted and the team sprinted over to beat the crowd and see whether they had made it. Anthony casually sauntered over a little behind the rest of them and when he didn't see his name, exclaimed in mock horror, "Oh no! And I soooo wanted to be in the finals too!"

After that first experience, I wasn't sure whether Anthony would want to continue, especially after reading one of his ballots, which stated, "There is a fine line between humor and BS and you definitely crossed it." To my surprise, he showed up to impromptu practice whenever the coach was there, gradually starting to write down his points and giving longer speeches with concrete evidence. Even with the new approach, he never stopped telling jokes, referencing his Swiss heritage, giving military examples, and providing personal stories, but somehow, over time, they seemed to work for him.

The final debate of the year was the novice invitational in May, and this time the wait at the subway station parking lot was almost luxurious. The sunlight removed the need for sweatshirts and enveloped us in its promise of summer. Instead of huddling around a cafeteria table while waiting for rounds, the Hillside team lounged outside on the grass or on top of the short brick wall surrounding the school. Suit jackets lay discarded on the lawn and ties were wrapped around their heads like bandanas. Anthony played the social butterfly once more, chatting up the girls and running races with the boys while his teammates cheered him on. The atmosphere was so laidback that the actual rounds themselves became an afterthought to the simple pleasures of hanging out with friends. Anthony didn't vent as much about these rounds, and I couldn't tell whether it was because he didn't care or because they were going well. My questions were answered when I watched his second speech on cyberbullying. "Today I'm going to talk to you about the problems with cyberbullying, such as (1) suicide, (2) federal charges, and (3) what our federal government is doing to crack down." I couldn't help but smile at his serious face and rigid posture, looking each audience member in the eye as he carefully outlined recent cyberbullying cases and the implications for society. "More and more people are doing this so the federal government is cracking down. Cybercrime units everywhere are looking for people who do these terrible things. Facebook itself has a feature to report cyberbullying. But it's still not enough. America needs people like you to point out that cyberbullying is wrong, and it's hurtful and it shouldn't happen. So I urge you to not cyberbully and tell people who do it that it's wrong. Thank you."

As we exited the room, Anthony quietly listened to me gush about his improvement. When he could tell I had finished, he turned to me, flashed a huge grin, and took off to join the next race with students from another school. He was so busy talking to everyone that he almost forgot to attend the awards ceremony at the end of the day. He had just entered the cafeteria when the announcer began listing the tournament finalists. Anthony was in the middle of telling a story to one of his teammates when I heard, "Anthony Gustafson." "Go up, go up Anthony! That's you!" "Me? What??" A stunned Anthony stumbled up to the front to accept his trophy, returning to the enthusiastic screams of the other Hillside debaters. They wouldn't even let him take his seat before nudging him out the door and jumping on him. "You won! You won! You're in varsity now! And you got a trophy!!" The 12 debaters ran off to the lawn on the side of the cafeteria, with me and the other researcher in tow. "Take our picture! Let's do a photo shoot jumping in the air!" It was a challenge to capture all of them up in the air as they jumped up and down, and by the end of it all, they collapsed on the ground in laughter, together with their newest varsity impromptu speaker.

Chapter 5

Pride and Possibility in Schools

When young people are used to being viewed in a certain way by society and the people they encounter every day, it is difficult for them to believe they can ever expect anything different from their experiences. They get better at predicting the eventual outcome of their efforts, even with little information—schoolwork will likely result in failing grades, leadership opportunities will always be just out of reach, and in an activity with a varsity division, they will remain in novice. Expanding the scope of possibilities available to them and convincing them that life can be different require a fundamental shift in how success is perceived as well as targeted efforts to disrupt existing deficit identities. Disability labels and school-based learning are not inherently restrictive; instead, whether pride is possible depends on how young people are treated, perceived, and positioned in culturally arranged contexts. The question of how to make strong, proud, academic identities possible is deeply embedded in "webs of significance" that shape conditions of power, difference, and community (Geertz, 1973; Peters, 2000). Markers of identity beyond disability (e.g., race, class, gender), and how these markers are perceived by others, mediate whether and how difference impacts individual freedom and well-being (Sen, 1992; Terzi, 2005). Repositioning youth and affirming positive identity require both individual and cultural change (Swain & French, 2000). As 15-year-old Colby Simpson points out in the quote that begins this section, "You need both the opportunity to grow and you need the courage to go out into the world and be yourself." Requiring more than occasional interventions with certain students, such change must take place in entire learning communities, where opportunities are offered to all students (not just the academic elite) and a shift in mindset about ability helps foster interactions that are supportive rather than punitive.

According to Thomas Hehir (2005), former director of the U.S. Department of Education's Office of Special Education Programs, the goal must be to "minimize the impact of disability and maximize the opportunities for children with disabilities to participate in general education in their natural community" (p.49). Such an approach reframes the question of how to cure disability as a question of how to alter social conditions so that disability is no longer associated with such dire consequences and is instead an aspect of human identity. Doing so emphasizes the distinction between disability as a part of identity and the formation of "disabled identities" as a result of marginalizing experiences. While this resembles the social model of disability in its focus on the role of cultural and environmental constraints, implementation must avoid "over-intellectualizing" the conversation to be more about social commentary than identifying resources for social action to actually address those constraints. Terzi (2005) argues that critical conversations about disability run the danger of "underspecifying what difference is . . . and failing to provide a definition of disability that can adequately inform the design of inclusive institutional and social schemes" (p. 203). This is not to say that conceptual framing is less important than practical action steps, but that they must be consciously linked. The way disability is defined, framed, and conceptualized must directly guide the kinds of questions asked, values and approaches prioritized, and assumptions made. It is not enough to believe that disability is an aspect of identity, without defining how specific dimensions of identity relate to suggested practices. Instead of becoming trapped in abstractions, conceptual ideas about ability must serve to construct concrete ways to expand opportunities, not only for the sake of equity, but to align with who young people are and who they want to be.

This chapter examines how a district alternative school in the Pacific Northwest (which I call Pathways Academy) attempts to address disabling social categorization by constructing a culture that supports diverse youth identities. While the racial demographics of its 140-student population were not diverse—83% of students were White—many came from special education and negative experiences in traditional schooling. Principal Hillary Collins stressed the fact that while 87% of students had had IEPs in their previous schools (largely for ADD/ADHD), only 18% were placed in special education at Pathways. "We did not want this to be seen as a special ed school," she reasoned. "We're not a special ed school even though we have many kids with disabilities. Instead, we just provide a flexible, supportive environment with accommodations already built-in for all students to take advantage of." In contrast to the experiences of James and Mark in the previous chapter, Pathways aimed to create a place where students could be proud of their identities, be comfortable with themselves, and have opportunities to develop confidence. For James and Mark, the perception that disability conflicted with both school expectations and their personal goals meant that they had to distance themselves either from disability or from the school setting itself. The case of Colby Simpson in this chapter considers other possibilities for youth pride through an examination of his participation in the school's "Music Workshop" collaboration between Pathways and former solo performing artists. His experience provides a starting point for exploring cultural change directed toward allowing students to embrace who they are while also opening up possibilities to discover something more.

SETTING THE STAGE: STEPPING INTO PATHWAYS

At 8:00 on a rainy weekday morning in the quiet Pacific Northwest town housing Pathways Academy, it was a familiar sight to see teenagers standing alone on street corners near the school quietly contemplating the day to come. With headphones in their ears, scowling expressions, and an occasional cigarette in hand, they could easily be mistaken for the clichéd images of angry-at-the-world, misunderstood adolescents that are so often the focus of news stories and TV dramas. Their outfits were trendy with an edge, with torn-up black T-shirts blazoned with band names atop skinny jeans, finished with slouchy knitted hats, piercings, and sometimes blue hair, all carefully composed to balance latest styles with their own individual stamp. Even Colby, with his sensibly cut blond hair, thick-framed glasses, and permanently cheery expression, wore all black, with the message "Keep Staring, I Might Do a Trick" etched on his T-shirt. At the stroke of 8:20, without the assistance of a school bell, the scattered individuals would pick up their artistically tattered leather shoulder bags or backpacks covered in political pins and patches and silently walk through the doors of Pathways Academy. Once inside, the piercings, black clothing, and "leave me alone" expressions were immediately contradicted by happy, cheery chatter. Instead of students huddled in small cliques, groups of adults and students gathered together, both graying and multicolored heads bent in collective discussion about politics, music, or career goals. And at the front door, greeting them all, was Principal Hillary Collins, a petite blond woman dressed in a neat suit and a huge smile whose high voice proclaimed warm welcomes to every new arrival. "Hello Colby! Hi Tina! Gabriella, it is so good to see you this morning! You all look wonderful—what a nice scarf, is it new? There's Tony! Our latest student of the week . . . I am so proud of you!"

Over the years, the walls and structure of the building have changed, but the welcome has not. Even when the school moved to a newly built, green energy building in the second year of fieldwork, its atmosphere remained supportive and personalized. In fact, the new structure brought the Pathways philosophy to life, with a large open gathering and performance space, specific classrooms devoted to the "Music Workshop" collaboration, "Healthy Living," environmental technology and design, 3-D design, weight training and yoga, woodwork, and student presentations. There was no cafeteria at Pathways; instead, adults and students ate together in rooms, stairwells, and hallways all over the school. Given the emphasis on sustainable energy and

green jobs, there were many occasions when students were outside school doing service learning at nearby sustainable businesses or local farms. According
to a 3rd-year student at Pathways, "Corporations look at us as leaders, not
just as kids . . . we are strong, mature adults who are good at something and
they are glad to have us." But even more than the freedom, choice, respect,
and love that was evident at the school, its culture was most often described
by students as "fearless." As opposed to experiences they had with bullying
and other "drama" prior to attending Pathways, many students stated that
they now could feel comfortable in their own skin. Comments such as, "I'm
not scared to ask questions anymore," "Teachers don't put me on the spot
and I'm not afraid to mess up," and, "It doesn't matter what people think
and I can perform in front of anyone!" were indicative of the confidence
fostered by school experiences. As one student elaborated, "I used to dread
school and it was like no one cared . . . not even the teachers. But here, the
teachers really want to help you with what you want to do and everyone likes
you for who you are. I can call myself a musician now and don't have to make
excuses for it."

FLEXIBLE SCHOOL STRUCTURES AND STUDENT PERCEPTIONS

Supporting student identities, building confidence, and battling negative histories in traditional schooling were not simply a matter of smiling
more, asking students about their day, or passing on a kind word or two.
Many Pathways students were deeply wounded by their experiences in traditional middle schools or comprehensive high schools, leading them to apply and transfer to Pathways in search of a fundamentally different approach
to schooling. While Pathways still had to meet the same state standards as
other district schools, the school model itself revolved around meeting district and graduation requirements through mentorship, service learning, flexibility and choice, counseling, and frequent feedback. As to the latter, the
traditional grading calendar was replaced with 15-day, credit-earning terms,
where students had to aim to reach a full "1.0" credit by meeting expectations in standards-based categories over 12 grading periods. As opposed to
receiving grades only per class, students could get partial credit toward the
1.0 by fulfilling expectations such as written literacy through a variety learning experiences and classes. The grading structure represented one of the
built-in accommodations for students diagnosed with disabilities, as students
received specific feedback focused on their personal learning goals every 15
days. Rather than being overwhelmed by falling behind in many areas, students were able to focus their work on small, manageable increments related
to their personal, identified goals.

Each credit term culminated in a celebration assembly with the entire school. The school day itself integrated student choice through a block-scheduled Friday, where students could go on career, art, and science fieldtrips; take culinary arts or professional music lessons; participate on the "Green Team" or "Leadership Team"; and take satellite courses through the community college. In contrast to its traditional counterparts, the Pathways model invested a great deal in counseling and mentorship, where all students would meet regularly with counselors about academic and personal issues, attend sessions specific to issues related to gender or drug prevention, and receive support from outside mentors during homeroom. Weekly staff meetings also had a fundamentally different feel, with a focus on supporting students' social and emotional needs. Teachers and leaders at the school were proud of their 98% attendance rate and 99% graduation rate, as well as the fact that 90% of students scored proficient in reading on state tests. At the same time, whereas Pathways focused on incorporating literacy and science through both in- and out-of-school experiences, educators struggled with finding a way to do the same in mathematics. Compared with the 90% proficiency rate in reading, only 19% of students scored proficient in math. Despite individual supports provided to students, math instruction was still largely remedial and less experiential, highlighting the importance of relational and real-world learning for Pathways students.

Beyond providing additional support for students, Pathways also had to face the challenge of battling negative perceptions of alternative schools. Contrary to outside perceptions that "troubled students" simply would be sent to school there, not everyone was admitted. Students had to fill out an application and a contract to be eligible for Pathways, and had to attend an intake interview, framed as a job interview, where incoming students set three goals they personally had for the year (which were then communicated to teachers). During my first visit to the school, students were extremely protective of Pathways and were quick to correct any misconceptions I might have. According to one student, "I chose to come here, not because of grades or behavior, but because I didn't like the style at my old school and I needed more individual attention. No one sent me here." Other students stressed that Pathways simply offered another option for students to explore their interests and "escape the drama of their past experiences." For Colby, Pathways provided a smaller, calmer environment to help him focus, connect with others, and manage the grand mal seizures he had suffered from since age 10. While interviews revealed intensely negative school experiences prior to Pathways, a schoolwide survey on youth perceptions of Pathways revealed that students felt that their teachers and peers valued their intelligence. Out of the total school population of 140 students, 70% of the 76 survey respondents thought that their peers saw them as "smart" and 98% felt that their teachers saw them as "a good student." Compared with the same survey results at the more traditional Hillside and Jefferson High Schools, half as many students (33.8%) said their families influenced what they wanted to do with their lives, with the biggest influence coming from outside mentors (likely due to the school's efforts to bring in outside professionals and provide all students access to them). In addition to outside support, a great deal of encouragement came from the teachers themselves. According to Principal Collins

> We don't let things go here, we sit down and talk about it. In general, kids here don't have strong support systems at home and we need to give it to them. At the same time, we build in flexibility within the district standards and we are sticklers for attendance. It is a choice and a privilege to come here.

Students recognized the value of attendance, identifying it as the most important factor in school success. When asked on the survey to rank the factors they thought teachers and administrators valued the most, attendance, completing assignments, and creativity and imagination topped the list (over test scores, going to college, and individuality). In fact, the biggest difference in school values was around test scores, with Hillside and Jefferson students perceiving tests as the most important value to teachers and administrator, and Pathways students ranking it as the least important. Another distinguishing feature of Pathways responses was that half of the respondents believed that "nobody" influenced their beliefs and values but themselves (as opposed to the overwhelming importance of family influence at Hillside and Jefferson). This individuality carried over to the types of career goals students identified, with beautician (14%), mechanic (9%), massage therapist (5%), and graphic designer (5%) as the most common careers. Hillside and Jefferson students, on the other hand, largely identified graduate school as their next career, along with engineering, medicine, and business. Overall, though, it is also worth noting that contrary to assumptions about teenagers being directionless, the majority of respondents at all schools answered that they had a clear idea of what they wanted to do as a career, but varied about whether schools supported their goals.

In contrast to the student experiences described earlier in this book, the Pathways model explicitly focused on how to encourage students to have personal pride and not feel the need to create distance from any aspect of their identities, as well as how to expand opportunities to develop confidence and skills related to students' goals. The personalized structure illustrated the desire to show students that they matter, even from the moment they enter the doors and the principal greets them by name. Class options were inspired by common life and skill goals of the student population, and the learning experience was individualized through explicit ties to individual learning goals and having multiple ways of fulfilling expectations so that students could play a role in the course of their education. Students stated that they felt valued at school in ways they were not at home, and various supports were put in place so that students would not feel marginalized (e.g., counseling, frequent feedback, teacher assistance targeting their goals). While students resented the negative perceptions they often received outside of school based on their appearance, they did not experience contradictions between school expectations and who they believed themselves to be.

Based on stories about their previous school experiences, most Pathways students would have fallen under the "creator" type of response, where they would disengage or withdraw from school and seek outside spaces to develop desired skills and abilities. As opposed to Tinsley and James, though, many of them did not have strong support from families or even the resources to pursue their interests and goals, making it even more important that Pathways provided experiences with outside professional mentors, service learning, satellite classes, and work placements. Since the entire school was designed as a community supporting student values, life goals, and perceptions of ability, they did not have to engage in different types of resistance to increase power over their lives. Their outside lives, goals, and identities were instead a central part of the learning process. Despite the socioemotional supports, the less rosy part of the picture in the eyes of more traditional educators might be whether simply attending school and completing work could qualify as high enough expectations for high school students. On a similar note, there were several occasions during the study where the research team questioned the content rigor, particularly in math classes. On the other hand, the fact that Pathways was able to instill such a deep sense of school pride and community for students who were previously so unhappy in school cannot be ignored. The tensions between promoting rigorous content and supporting academic identity development beg the question of how "success" should be defined and what school values should be.

COLBY SIMPSON: COMING BACK TO LIFE

Even when the design of school structures and perceptions of the majority broadly support inclusive ideals, it often can be difficult to grasp important social dynamics solely through surveys or narratives of school design. The nuances of individual experiences and personal histories play a crucial role in exploring the potential for cultural change in entire learning communities. For Colby Simpson, the journey to Pathways Academy was a complex blur of bullying, "spacing out," severe meltdowns, and seizures. Even from his early years, his mother, Maggie, remembered him always being more of an observer than a participant in school activities. Although it comforted Maggie to have a label for Colby's condition after going through disability testing in 1st grade, it did not help his position as an outsider. Being labeled with epilepsy and a "nonverbal learning disability"on the autism spectrum made him feel like an "other" and he started to socially withdraw even further. His speech impediment, regular grand mal seizures, and gentle nature made him the primary target for bullies in both elementary and middle school. Maggie recalled having to change elementary schools three times because, rather than offering necessary support, his teachers would complain about having to deal with such a high-maintenance kid with serious health issues. Similar to the case of Anthony's mother Greta mentioned in A Mother's Tale, Maggie often felt alienated by the rest of the parents at all of Colby's schools because she advocated for him so often before the board. Instead of becoming resentful, in 6th grade Colby started taking on the role of the "silent advocate." He quietly persisted in asking for help from adults (even when they did not want to help him), and did not get overly preoccupied with trying to fit in with his peer group. He viewed bullies without malice and did not believe they wanted to actually cause him pain. "They are just different than me," he would tell his mother when she would talk to him about not being a victim. "They just don't see the world like me."

After his seizures worsened in middle school, Maggie and Colby sought out Pathways, which was offering 7th and 8th grades at the time (it has since shifted to only grades 9–12). After a year of attending Pathways and enjoying the professional instrumental lessons, Colby started saying he no longer wanted to continue. Although he appreciated the difference in teacher support, he continued to encounter boys who made fun of him during and in-between classes. He found a community with a group of older girls in his music classes, but since it was the first year of Pathway's founding, negative perceptions of alternative schools remained, even among students. The goal was still to be "mainstreamed," which would signify true success because the students believed they would no longer be outsiders. After 1 year, Colby enrolled in another regular middle school, where the large class sizes, noisy confusing hallways, and stress of changing classes triggered constant grand mal seizures. While Maggie worried about Colby's lethargy and health, he continued to say he did not want special education classes because they were boring and he did not want to stand out further. Midway through the year, Colby returned to Pathways, because, in short, "regular school was bad for his health."

This time around, Colby recognized and appreciated having the time to be able to process information, especially in contrast to the second regular middle school, which was overwhelmingly fast-paced in everyday interactions. He began taking culinary arts, volunteering to cater an event to get "another notch in his belt." Despite participating in more new activities, Colby had fewer seizures, and they continued to decrease significantly with each year. Maggie worried that he would not be capable of completing many of these experiences, only to have Colby remind her, "I need to take risks." The risk-taking continued to one of the satellite programs, which trained students for green energy jobs. Before attending his first session, the school (and particularly George, his special education teacher) helped Colby communicate his needs to the company representatives, informing them that he needed to slowly ramp up his learning and not become too overstimulated. George elaborates:

> Confidence. He sees himself as a person who is capable of achieving anything he puts his mind to; whether he gets it or not, he's willing to try. He is extremely empathetic, he cares deeply for others, he goes out of his way to help people. He is extremely sensitive and has been hurt many times by people who misunderstand what he says or how he says it. Some people are mean or tactless and it hurts, and instead of keeping it in, now he's more willing to seek out an adult and get help. I think he's learned to trust adults.

Unfortunately, his new, inclusive experience did not always extend to his peers. While the culture at Pathways now had more of a sense of school pride and community (as opposed to before, when everyone wanted to be mainstreamed), Colby still had trouble feeling accepted by other students. Even though he was a hard worker, students would distance themselves from Colby when it was time to choose groups. During a fieldtrip activity in the nearby woods, for instance, one of his group members even lured Colby to look at a collection of brush and shrubbery, calling it the "bat house." While Colby went to investigate, the boy said to the rest of the group, "Quick! Let's run off and leave him!" In class, his teachers appreciated his growing confidence and willingness to participate when others were quiet. What he had to try to ignore, though, were the constant snickers from three boys in the back of the room. When the teachers noticed it, they reminded everyone that students were all expected to participate and spoke with individual troublemakers about not laughing at Colby. Instead of stopping, the boys simply got better at disguising their teasing so that their comments or actions could not be directly tied to Colby, but it was clear to Colby that they were making fun of him. They walked around with their mouths open like Colby often would, making sure he would see them. When Colby would try to tell jokes in class, they would look at one another meaningfully and simply say, "awkward Thursday." On one of these occasions in algebra class during groupwork, the teacher was working with students individually, and the boys were staring at one another intensely and then staring at Colby with their mouths open. They mumbled comments under their breath and burst out laughing.

> BOY 1: . . . if he stares at you for too long, he'll probably touch you and get all weirded out.
> BOY 2: Yeah, he probably didn't take his meds today.
> COLBY: (from across the room) You know, I would appreciate it if you didn't talk about me behind my back.
> BOYS 1 AND 2: (overlapping protests to the teacher) We didn't! We didn't say anything rude . . .
> COLBY: You don't know what's rude and what's not.
> TEACHER: Don't talk about people behind their back.
> BOY 2: We weren't! (looking around the room) Did anyone hear me say something bad?
> COLBY: You don't know what's perceived badly and what's not. (goes back to work)
> COLBY: (after a few minutes of everyone working alone silently, turns to the teacher) What do I need to do good in this class? Is it going okay, am I missing any work?

Later on in an interview, Colby discussed his relationships with other students, saying, "Sometimes, it feels like people don't give me a chance, probably, and they aren't very understanding. They have this impression of me and they always say something snarky. But they are just annoying because they are just trying to be part of the conversation." In counseling sessions and conversations with George, his special education teacher, he was encouraged to embrace his own individuality, not feel the pressure to conform to other people's expectations, and become part of the advocacy process and more of a participant in his future. He expressed a desire to learn how to be comfortable showing his "true side" to people. He believed in George's advice, that "sometimes, you just gotta jump in and try something out. That's part of what life is, jumping in blind." He continued:

> The teachers at Pathways allow me to do that. I get to try new things and it's really a build up for me to go out into the world after I'm done here and try out whatever I'm going to do, whether that be music or cooking or . . . I've been doing sports too, like baseball. It's given me the opportunity to grow. I honestly think if I was in a mainstream school I would have gotten lost and the reason why I left my old middle school was my meds but the teachers noticed me because they could see I was

trying and it just wasn't a good fit. And I appreciate them doing that for me and suggesting for me to come back here. It was a turning point. I went from not really appreciating Pathways because I didn't know what anything else was at that point to realizing the uniqueness of it. I just appreciate everything Pathways has done for me.

Still, Colby wished that everyone could believe in him. Even when he learned to advocate for himself and felt like he "could do anything," he continued to feel like the same quiet observer he had been in elementary school. He had the confidence and was no longer afraid to make mistakes, but what was the cost of making mistakes in the eyes of his peers? And in public performances, was it really okay to make mistakes? Given that acceptance was so important to him, he continued to face an ongoing tension between meeting the social expectations of others and simply saying, as he often did, "I am who I am, and I am game for anything."

MENTORSHIP AT THE MUSIC WORKSHOP

To many people, being accepted might mean conformity or at least flying below the radar in terms of any behavior that could be construed as "abnormal." To LaShonda Evans, acceptance meant handing a person a microphone. As the primary musical instructor at the Pathways Music Workshop and a former Las Vegas R&B and Motown singer, she believed strongly that young people should never think of themselves as victims and instead should feel a sense of pride that they could celebrate on stage. The Music Workshop was an even more intensely supportive subculture of Pathways, where "it is all about where you are right now and you don't have to make apologies for anything." While new students were often shy around LaShonda's fierce and passionate style, her love was contagious. Students found themselves using her language, saying to one another, "I care about you, you can do it!" "Don't back down!" "You are beautiful, we want to hear your voice!" According to Colby, "It's easy to build a relationship with LaShonda because she enjoys us, the way we enjoy her. She's so open with everyone and treats everyone the same, like family." He often would note how in Music Workshop more people would talk to him, not only because they were mostly girls (and not the same boys who would tease him in math) but also because "LaShonda shows us how to care."

Beyond her everyday interactions with students, LaShonda was able to promote youth pride through a strong collaboration with Bill, a retired Pathways teacher who started the program, connected with LaShonda and other solo performing artists, and handled the management. Between LaShonda's

Las Vegas connections and Bill's organizational skills, they were able to book performances for the students at prestigious music clubs and performance spaces. As LaShonda would say, "This ain't just your typical show in the community center." At performances, they would hire professional make-up artists and rent costumes (again through connections), which made the experience more authentic and real for students. And she featured Colby in many solos, complete with choreography. According to Colby's mother:

> The Music Workshop brought him back to life . . . I saw a Colby I had never seen before, it was like watching a birth. Everyone had stopped him from performing before until Pathways. It wasn't really about the music for Colby. He didn't need his meds as much and we started tapering it off. He celebrates the fact that he has value. He is more savvy and less hypersensitive (he used to cry all the time when his feelings were hurt), and he started becoming more compassionate. When I saw my kid on stage, feeling it—living life out loud, finally—I was so proud, beaming . . . it gave me goose bumps and it gave us hope. We had just accepted things, that he would just not be excited about life.

More than simply providing instructional supports or offering class material that connected to students' interests, the Music Workshop tapped into students' emotions and taught them how to speak with one another. Teachers at the school recognized how the Music Workshop was not just an elective, but an essential part of helping the school build its culture and fulfill its goals in terms of socioemotional supports. As George put it, "[Colby] was accepted as a group member fully and completely, not just, let's put a token person here. Everyone is a full partner. They might not get the microphone, but everyone is important. He could say, people know who I am and people accept me for who I am." The community experience did not simply end after each Music Workshop session was over, but extended to its participants' everyday class interactions, where students would stand up for one another, "for our family."

After one particularly strong run-through of a "Circle of Life," everyone was in tears, including both Bill and LaShonda. Huddled together, they gave thanks for their community.

> LaShonda: It's so rewarding to work with and for people and it works. There's nothing like giving up yourself and it's appreciated and fabulous. You're singing like your hearts are open—that's what made me cry . . . I want you to be good singers, but I want your hearts open—it makes me feel proud to have something to do with that, with your hearts being open.

STUDENT: I didn't want to come to school today, but I did for this.

COLBY: This is my CPR for the day. I watch the clock in math class, looking forward to this. You're all the reason I'm less nervous, less scared.

STUDENT: I used to hate choir at my old school, I stood in the back so no one would see me.

LASHONDA: You're not in the back anymore baby! (everyone cries even more and Colby pumps his fist in the air)

LASHONDA: Don't let anyone change what you know is good and right— never let anyone define your experience for you, cuz what if they're wrong? You sing, and everyone will adjust to you.

Giving thanks for their community and the opportunity to make music was not uncommon at the Music Workshop, and Colby often stated that it was the reason that he stopped wanting to go to mainstream schools. "I'm unique and I have more here than I would there," he would argue. Rather than feeling insecure when his peers would judge or underestimate him, he instead took their teasing as a challenge. He elaborated:

There's nothing you can do because people are going to underestimate you no matter what, you have to show them . . . that's why I'm in the Music Workshop, I want to show people who I am and that it's not just music, it's putting a little bit of your soul too, on the line. I think of myself as a performer. There could have been a time when I didn't think so, but I've grown as a musician and a person over the past few years. I don't want to give that up.

ACCESSIBILITY AND CAPABILITIES

As often noted in disability studies literature, the nature of the cultural context and human relationships determine the importance assigned to disability and whether it has relevance in that context (e.g., Campbell & Oliver, 1996; Peters, 2000). Inclusive values cannot merely be mandated but must involve people who are directly involved in the experiences in question (Sen, 1999). In the case of Pathways, encouraging students to take pride in themselves and in others was not simply a matter of putting such values in its mission statement or even training teachers to implement inclusive practices. The values needed to be embedded within the culture of the school itself, from adults like LaShonda modeling how to interact with one another to students learning how to advocate for themselves and for others. They not only needed to know that it was important to support one another, but they had to truly

believe it. Having a disability needed to become something that did not automatically imply "otherness" but instead was an aspect of personal identities
that could become a natural part of the school's collective identity (Swain &
French, 2000). Taking action to encourage the affirmation of positive identity required the school and members of its community to do as disability
activist Fran Branfield (1999) argues: "define who one is fighting for, what
our values are, and how one wants to bring about change" (p. 401).

As opposed to many disabled people's movements, which advocate for
the "celebration of difference" (Terzi, 2005), Pathways was distinct in that
it instead focused on celebrating the collection of individual identities that
made up the school community. For Colby, conversations around his Pathways experience revolved less around specifically taking pride in his disability
and were more about accepting all parts of his self, feeling supported by others, and having opportunities to celebrate his identity. Opportunities such as
the Music Workshop mirrored the capabilities perspective in the literature, by
helping extend the capabilities that could "amount to the substantive freedoms a person has or the 'real alternatives' available to the person to achieve
well-being" (Sen , 1992, p. 41). In this way, the educational experience itself
could expand the set of capabilities that students could choose from. Options
at Pathways also linked directly to students' identified life and career goals,
supporting students' decisions about leading different kinds of lives. More
than focusing on students' intrinsic abilities, the structure of Pathways framed
"ability as agency," where students were engaged in learning for the purpose
of expanding their future options, surpassing their own learning goals, and
empowering their sense of pride in the process. This is consistent with studies
by Watson (2002), which suggest that developing pride in a disability identity
is contingent upon individuals and communities defining disability on their
own terms, and defining themselves first and foremost as people. Rather than
acting more like the boys in Colby's algebra class who reacted primarily to his
superficial appearance and behavior, adults and students in the Music Workshop were able to appreciate and celebrate who Colby was as a person and as
a performer. His case helps illustrate the need to understand how identities
develop (Darling, 2003) and the potential that schools can have as places
where identities are promoted through broader community supports.

Regardless of the negative school experiences that Pathways students had
before arriving at the school, they were all supported in "rejecting the stigma
that there is something sad or to be ashamed of in their condition" (Shapiro,
1994, p. 20). Adults and students alike vehemently rejected the perceptions
of alternative high school students as "pitiable victims" and instead took pride
in their identities. As Peters (2000) points out, it is important for individuals
with disabilities to claim a cultural identity and establish themselves as "active
agents of transformation beyond objectified and marginalized Others" (p.

585). Being bullied, failing school, or simply not being able to learn in a limited and restrictive way may once have defined how they viewed themselves as students, but as soon as they entered Pathways, they were presented with a new set of possibilities.

It is tempting to write off the example of Pathways Academy as a unique and singular case impossible to replicate, particularly due to its small size, outside connections and community partnerships, and lack of racial and economic diversity. While these factors indeed might have played a role in making the Pathways school culture a reality, it is important not to let "yes, but . . ." statements act as excuses to ignore cultural ideals that can be actionable or disregard such a culture as a valuable aspiration. More than anything, the mindset of using education as a means to increase students' control over the direction of their lives was extremely powerful in terms of alleviating cultural, learning, and opportunity barriers that might have interfered with their personal goals. Similarly, the approach of designing an entire school environment to anticipate student needs and be universally supportive of those needs was fundamentally different from isolating single students who might not be learning as fast, or identifying them for individual interventions. Consistency and community among the adults was also important in terms of enacting Pathways ideals, and they modeled inclusive behavior by building a sense of community among themselves and genuinely liking and respecting one another. Balancing a culture of support with multiple opportunities to explore strengths helped promote students' confidence and the courage to exert command over their experiences and take back control over their lives.

And through it all, the adults were only a small piece of facilitating the possibility of pride. While LaShonda provided the foundation and modeled ideal practices, at the end of the day students were the ones who did the singing, creating and living out the community with one another. It was no surprise that their favorite song was Des'ree's "You Gotta Be," which they sometimes would spontaneously sing huddled together in a circle at the end of practice.

> Remember, listen as your day unfolds, challenge what the future holds, try and keep your head up to the sky. Lovers, they may cause you tears, go ahead release your fears. . . . You gotta be bad, you gotta be bold, you gotta be wiser. You gotta be hard, you gotta be tough, you gotta be stronger. You gotta be cool, you gotta be calm, you gotta stick together. All I know, all I know, love will save the day.

Chapter 6

Supporting Ability Development in Classrooms

Teachers can play a powerful role in repositioning youth who historically are marginalized in schools. While disrupting deficit identities ultimately requires broader cultural transformation, expanding the scope of possibilities for all students is still possible even in the absence of schoolwide structural changes. Doing so requires overall supports to help students exercise individuality, opportunities for active participation, and, most important, a flexible, ability-oriented mindset driven by detailed information about who they are as people and learners. Fortunately, in each case mentioned so far, the students had a few teachers, friends, family members, administrators, and activities that helped them feel like they could live out their identities proudly and develop abilities that could drive their desired life directions. The dynamics that facilitated the expansion of active participation were complex and shifted over time, sometimes in subtle ways. The more positive relationships and experiences were characterized by more expansive and inclusive definitions of success and intelligence, whereas the subjective nature of ability was recognized by both adults and other students. While the Pathways case was one of the more apparent examples of how instructors appreciated a nuanced picture of ability, Devin Foster's teammate Katie went through a similar realization when she discovered that different teachers could bring out different pictures of success from Devin. Success was not solely a matter of Devin's individual effort or intrinsic potential, but a complex interplay of human interactions. Katie's realization that "success" was malleable allowed her to appreciate Devin's capabilities as a debater.

Both in and outside of school, all of the learning environments that captivated the students were flexible, with built-in opportunities for choice and active participation. From James Ovill's nature trips to Anthony's involvement in the police shadowing program, there were plentiful chances to develop students' ability to teach others and act as leaders. It would not have been possible to direct their own learning if it were not for having a safe space (like Tinsley's world of creative writing) and community where they felt appreciated and could display their strengths (as with Colby in the

Music Workshop). Similar to Spencer's appreciation of his debate coach's approach to team building, being around a diverse group of people provided an important and valuable backdrop to living inclusive experiences. In the area of specific implementation of inclusive experiences, qualities of empowering spaces included whole-child supports (e.g., socioemotional and academic scaffolds), whole-life supports (both across settings and over time), explicit instructional accommodations with immediate opportunities to apply new skills, and language that modeled inclusive behavior. On a broader level, empowering experiences offered time, opportunity, and social resources to develop practice-linked identities through authentic discovery. Students did not have to wait to explore different possibilities for their lives, and received advance preparation for failure and disappointment in case they were not able to fulfill the image they had for themselves, such as with Mark Browning and his special education teacher, Ms. Hayes. Given the incredible range of experiences, interactions, and environments that supported youth ability development, though, "teachers are neither the saviors nor the culprits" (Fischer & Forester, 1993). The point of these observations is not to say teachers are solely responsible for repositioning young people, only that a shift in mindset regarding youth success and potential can go a long way toward doing so.

This chapter discusses overall supports that must be put in place to help students exercise their power and individuality, even in a traditional classroom setting. Since teachers can play a central role in challenging or reproducing disablement, the chapter focuses on establishing a mindset to reposition and empower youth, along with concrete tools to drive a practical theory of change. Neither the school setting nor disability itself inherently means that students would be negatively positioned, but several key external factors can serve to restrict youth participation. Throughout this book, bias and academic stereotypes about who could succeed often drove classroom interactions, sometimes based purely on race, gender, or past behavior. More generally, a dearth of information about students could lead to misperceptions of both their capabilities and actions in the classroom. A lack of awareness of students' lives outside of school not only contributed to a deeper chasm between students' multiple worlds but also kept schools from truly appreciating and expanding upon the complex learning practices students would independently pursue. This was part of why students had fewer opportunities to explore their individual goals at school, especially students who were not perceived as worthy of "enrichment" experiences. Contradictions between youth goals and teacher concerns resulted in different patterns in youth resistance in an effort to expand their agency and fight back against social restrictions on their participation. And in the face of negative positioning, students too often were left on their own, leading to the development of fragmented identities where they had no choice but to distance themselves from school or aspects of themselves that were not perceived as "normal." While many educational interventions aim to target aspects of these issues (such as extensive efforts in science education to build on students' outside lives), the conversation is rarely framed in terms of how to critique and un-learn disabling practices.

AN ABILITY-ORIENTED MINDSET FOR TEACHING

Instructional mindsets that promote ability development in service of youth agency must begin with a close look at how success and intelligence are de-fined in the learning setting and how each student relates to these cultural definitions. It is not enough to tacitly accept broader, institutionally driven beliefs about who can succeed in school, even when they are deeply embed-ded in the culture of schooling. National and state standards do not inher-ently imply visions of school success that alienate students with disabilities. Instead, it is in how standards and content are delivered that subjective per-ceptions of ability sometimes can take on a more sinister form. In short, a mindset for teaching must be ability-oriented, considering how students can develop strengths that meet their goals and needs. Such a mindset necessar-ily must revolve around how teachers can gather specific evidence, data, and information about young people, including what they can do (instead of just what they can't do and what needs to be fixed). As informed by the student cases mentioned in earlier chapters, ability-oriented mindsets for teaching must consider the following kinds of questions:

- How can educators avoid making judgments or having negative per-ceptions about students based on little information about who they are?
- What would it look like in practice to embrace abilities as a means for students to exercise agency and power over their lives?
- What approaches can help bridge any gaps between student goals and teacher priorities?
- What tools and resources can collect additional evidence about envi-ronmental barriers to learning, rather than blaming the student for failure?
- How can educators collect better data to understand who students are in terms of identity, instead of stopping at surface-level back-ground information?
- How can educators open up more opportunities for active and per-sonalized participation that emphasizes student voice, expression, and leadership?

- How can educators support students by anticipating their needs, helping them through the entire learning process, and building in (from the beginning) universal, class- and schoolwide accommodations?

Even if there are no clear answers to these kinds of questions, the mere attempt to investigate youth experiences in this way helps alleviate the contradictions that drive youth to resist as challengers, creators, and rebels. The goal is not to eliminate the existence of youth resistance to social positioning dynamics, especially since such active responses provide young people with a way of exploring different identities and exercising their agency. Instead, the goal should be not to leave young people entirely alone in this process or forever positioned in a way that requires them to withdraw from school altogether. The focus must be on addressing the root of their reactions to disabling practices. Their resistance to disablement is not the problem (although it often manifests in disruptive behavior that is treated as such), but rather how the disconnect between school learning and their lives results in misperceptions, missed opportunities, and mistaken assumptions about ability.

Not addressing the types of questions listed above would have direct consequences for students who are attempting to resist disabling practices. For the students in this book, the assumption that teacher priorities necessarily would match what students cared about resulted in several types of resistance responses. They included withdrawal behavior from "creator" students, who felt the need to create their own safe space, and from "rebels," who resented school expectations, along with intensive energy and time spent by "challengers," who wanted to fit definitions of success. Focusing more on how students were responsible for academic failure (as opposed to environmental barriers) led "creators" like Tinsley and James to perceive school as not conducive to the development of personal passions, and "rebels" like Anthony and Spencer to feel as though they were not seen as having valuable goals. Not having the opportunity to develop personal talents in school would raise the stakes for students to find access and support outside of school, and jeopardize their identities if they were unable to do so. Not recognizing academic stereotypes would be especially difficult for "challengers" such as Devin and Mark, especially when left unsupported in dealing with academic failure that could so threaten their self-perception of being high-achieving students. The lack of opportunities for active participation could lead to the belief, on the part of all students, that school was not connected to their interests, their voices were not valued, or they could not be trusted to handle leadership roles. Given the social and subconscious ways that disablement is present in schools, even individual teacher efforts to challenge rigid ideas about what students can do and how they learn, can offer at least one safe and supportive space for strong academic identities to develop.

From Ability Framing to Everyday Practice

First steps toward supporting ability development in classrooms require improved information-gathering systems, supports informed by knowledge of student strengths, and a focus on bridging any gaps between teacher concerns and student goals. More specifically, information-gathering systems must collect more evidence about student strengths and ways to incorporate explicit opportunities for youth leadership in the classroom. Improved assessments require targeted ways of asking questions about student abilities and needs both pre- and post-instruction. Any supports designed must then be connected to knowledge about students and any specific barriers to learning, and should be present throughout the entire learning process (rather than being added on as an extra section on accommodations). Doing this requires organization systems for documenting student strengths, needs, and goals over time in an effort to relate students' personal goals to teacher concerns. The central question that connects all of these methods is, "How can instruction be designed to support students in developing abilities that will serve their needs, goals, and future life directions?" This question is substantially different from more teacher-focused questions such as, "How can students meet my objectives?" or "How can I catch up students who are falling behind state standards?" In the latter two questions, students are inherently positioned as failing, or somehow in the wrong, needing to somehow change what they are doing (or even who they are) to fit expectations. The first question instead is focused on how school learning can better serve students by improving their lives, engaging their interests, and, ultimately, expanding their opportunities and options in life. School achievement then becomes a vehicle for increasing youth agency, rather than an end in itself. While many of the ideas listed above are not new, they take on a different form when framed as a way to address expanding youth agency over the learning process and changing deficit-oriented beliefs.

The three tools presented in the following sections of the chapter are suggested examples for approaching many of the aforementioned questions. Each of these tools was inspired by the students in this book and designed with their concerns and challenges in mind to help make the process of "unlearning disability" more concrete. The first is a matrix, which aims to lead teachers through a process of anticipating student needs, making accommodations, and designing ways to collect additional evidence. This matrix was driven particularly by the cases of Tinsley Hawkins and Devin Foster, to help gather more evidence about a quiet student like Tinsley, or specifically target individual struggles with support (like the intervention at the debate tournament with Devin). The second tool is a version of a lesson plan template, which not only models how students need supports throughout the entire learning process but also involves coming up with opportunities for active participation. The template was designed after meeting James, Spencer, and Anthony, who needed curriculum and instruction to better address their life goals and provide more chances for them to demonstrate and showcase their leadership abilities. Finally, the third tool is a reflection and recording grid to help quickly document student strengths, needs, and a variety of identified goals over time. Mark and Colby informed this chart based on the need to better keep track of their developing strengths (which often went missed in the classrooms), as well as the desire to collect more information about their personal goals (as opposed to allowing them to try to fit into the goals other people had for them). All of these tools are intended only as examples that can be adjusted and changed based on individual classroom needs and contextual realities, and are by no means the only possibilities for addressing the questions listed above.

STUDENT-INFORMED TEACHING:
A MATRIX FOR ACCOMMODATIONS AND ASSESSMENTS

This matrix, shown in Figure 6.1, treats instructional accommodations and assessments as connected, rather than two separate parts of the planning process. It is based on the argument that to come up with appropriate supports for learning, a teacher must have gathered specific evidence and information about student needs and potential barriers, as well as student strengths. Since well-designed assessments help monitor student learning, they provide a means for constantly informing supports. Not only do they target specific student needs, but assessments also provide more information about who students are, avoiding unfounded assumptions or misperceptions about their behavior. The matrix goes row-by-row and takes teachers through the pre-instruction, instruction, and post-instruction stages of teaching, a process that inevitably involves a constant cycle of thinking about instructional approaches and actually "doing" them.

After using this matrix with a group of 100 preservice teachers, we found that the easiest boxes to answer were those in column A, around using knowledge of students to anticipate barriers. The more difficult questions were those asking teachers to consider how they were learning about and utilizing student strengths, as well as providing opportunities for students to express what they knew. In discussion, the teacher candidates pointed to the fact that schools so often focus on what students (especially those with disabilities) do not know or where they fall behind. Strengths and talents are

FIGURE 6.1. Matrix for Accommodations and Assessments

	A — Use knowledge of students by... **Anticipating Barriers**	B — Support progress and access by... **Creating Accommodations**	C — Gather evidence of meeting objectives by... **Assessing**	Teacher **Think/Do Steps**	
1	Where will students struggle with different parts of the lesson?	How can I specifically target their struggle with support?	How will I know if my supports actually will help?	*Thinking:* Getting started	preinstruction
2	*Note the following:* "Given the lesson, who might struggle, why might they struggle, and what strengths do they have that can be built upon?"	*Write on plan:* "For students who struggle with ____, I plan to . . ."	*Write on plan:* "I will check for understanding by looking for ____ and listening for ____ to see if students are meeting the objectives."	*Doing:* Lesson planning	
3	How might their strengths and interests help address barriers?	How do I think these accommodations will help?	How am I giving them opportunities to express what they know?	*Thinking:* Justification process	instruction
4	*During instruction:* Gather more information about specific struggles and strengths.	*During instruction:* Observe students who were anticipated to struggle.	*During instruction:* Collect evidence specifically geared toward measuring how students are meeting objectives.	*Doing:* Getting the evidence	
5	Did their strengths and interests help address barriers? Why or why not?	Did the accommodations help? Why or why not?	How do I know whether the accommodations helped?	*Thinking:* Reflecting	postinstruction
6	*Next time:* "Prior to this lesson, certain students struggled with ____. Here is where they made progress and why. They still struggle with ____."	*Next time:* "I accommodated their learning needs by ____. For the next lesson, I plan to . . ."	*Next time:* "I will continue to know if students are making progress toward their learning goals by looking for ____ and listening for ____."	*Doing:* Figuring out next steps	

left to be expressed and developed outside of school, whereas they actually can be used to address areas of need in school. Teachers commented on how difficult it was to actively collect information about student talents outside of school, as well as to connect plans with specific areas of struggle beyond a disability label or outside behavior. The statement, "For students who struggle with ___, I plan to . . . " was not how they typically were asked in their districts to create accommodations; instead, they were asked simply to list the supports mentioned in their individualized education plans. The idea that any action could become an accommodation, as long as it served the purpose of specifically addressing a learning need or barrier, was unusual and went beyond the overall disability label and diagnosis. The teacher candidates also had to think about specific behavior or language they were "looking for" and "listening for," instead of reacting to student behavior in the moment, which sometimes can lead to misperceptions. This matrix aims to encourage the collection of as much information as possible to inform planning, instruction, and, most important, student–teacher interactions.

ACTIVE AND SUPPORTED PARTICIPATION: PLANNING FOR BARRIERS AND OPPORTUNITIES

The lesson plan template in Figure 6.2 illustrates the process of anticipating student needs, designing accommodations, and facilitating active student opportunities throughout every step of the lesson plan process. Built on the theory of Universal Design for Learning (Rose & Meyer, 2002), the underlying idea is that goals, materials, activities, and assessments must all be flexible and accessible, and that accommodations must be incorporated from the very beginning. This is different from typical lesson plan templates, which often add "accommodations" or "modifications to the lesson" as a separate section. The difficulty with this approach is that it encourages teachers (particularly new teachers) to think of instructional supports in a vacuum or to isolate students with disabilities as the only ones in need of support. The template in Figure 6.2 instead asks teachers to come up with goals and then immediately think about who might struggle with those goals and about how they can come up with supports that specifically target goal-related barriers. They can then apply these supports to all students, rather than singling out individual students as the only ones with problems, which can position them as having lower status in the classroom. Similarly, the column for "opportunities" requires teachers to consider how, in each aspect of the lesson, students can be asked to play a more active role in their learning. "Opportunities" can refer to any action or activity that has students making discoveries, acting as leaders, engaging in decisionmaking or making choices, becoming teachers,

FIGURE 6.2. Lesson Plan Template

	Plan	Barriers	Accommodations	Opportunities
Goals/Driving Questions:				
Objective(s):				
Assessment: • How will you know when you have achieved your goals for most students? Who will still struggle? • How will you help students express what they know, regardless of disability?				
Skills: • What are the "desirable struggles" on this day? • What skills are also required to complete tasks but are not the central focus, and how can you alleviate these struggles?				
Materials: • When is text appropriate? • How do you help scaffold that text? • When could something else be used to represent the material?				
Activities: • How can you help make the instructions clearer? • How can you help make the learning process more concrete (e.g., graphic organizers)?				

or asking proactive questions (as opposed to simply responding to teacher directives or listening). Once again, every aspect of the lesson can contain opportunities for active, student-led learning, and the flow of the template shows how barriers can be supported with accommodations to provide opportunities for developing strengths and talents. Although this template contains many of the same ingredients as a traditional lesson plan, the process of thinking itself uses a mindset of adjusting the lesson and classroom environment to address potential barriers, rather than seeing the student as at fault if something does not go as planned. Blaming students for failure not only positions them as "bad students," but also leads to students' perception that they constantly will be unable to learn or somehow be restricted in their participation in that particular class.

The theme of this template is how different aspects of the learning process or environment can be clarified or better customized to support all students, with or without disabilities. The guiding questions under "skills" focus on "desirable difficulties," which refer to what Rose and Meyer (2006) call the specific struggles that a teacher wants students to work on during a particular day. Too often, students are asked to struggle with the full range of skills and content that eventually will be required of them, rather than focusing on a few central skills at a time. Other peripheral skills often can interfere with students being able to express that they have mastered the central skill or can even get in the way of the learning itself. This can be related to specific disability needs, but also can be the case for any student in the class. For instance, in group presentations, a teacher might be more interested in the content and in how students have demonstrated their mastery of the subject of choice. However, a student who struggles with presentation and delivery skills may have trouble showing that she has learned the content. The presentation skills become the "undesirable difficulty" that gets in the way of the material the teacher wants her to struggle with. On a different day, the central focus skill might be the act of writing a five-paragraph essay, and navigating dense text to read the supplemental text material might be the "undesirable difficulty." The same difficulty—reading complex text—that is "undesirable" on that day might be the central focus skill in a different lesson. Any skill can be an undesirable difficulty on any given day, if it is not one of the central focus struggles. "Desirable" and "undesirable" difficulties can change daily, depending on the focus of the lesson. The difference is that students who know how to play the game of school can tell "what the teacher is looking for," whereas it can be less clear to others. By making this distinction explicit to all students, teachers play a key role in filtering difficulties for students, alleviating some of the frustrations that can lead to disruptive behavior or eventual negative perceptions of student ability and potential.

DEVELOPING STRENGTHS AND GOALS:
A REFLECTION AND DOCUMENTATION GRID

One of the most difficult aspects of implementing ability-oriented approaches is how to find time and resources to synthesize so much information. Given the amount of planning and reflection required from these tools, it can be overwhelming to have to write and record evidence for a large number of students in the limited amount of time in between classes or before the next day. The following grid aims to provide an example of one organization system that can act as a low-maintenance approach to recording student strengths, needs, and goals. It requires little writing, and instead is more a means of viewing the big picture of the class population. Each entire grid represents a single class, or however often the teacher wants to record information. It first asks the teacher to list three focus skills that are covered during an extended period of time in the class (e.g., week, month, or full unit). For each student, the teacher can then reflect on how students are performing around each skill, writing a 1 if the skill is an area of significant struggle, and a 5 indicating an area of particular strength. After looking at several grids, a teacher could get a general picture of whether a student is experiencing all 1s and struggling with all focal skills, or whether there is any place where he demonstrates strengths. Ideally, all students would have at least one 4 or 5, where they are able to not only display their strengths for the class but also build upon them in order to better support the other areas that they struggle with. Since this is not often the case given the context of certain lessons, documenting different skills over time may eventually provide a way of noticing when there is a student strength in a particular area, which the teacher can then utilize more often in future lessons.

The second half of the grid allows teachers to document students' personal, academic, life, and future goals, hopefully helping them consider how teacher priorities align (or do not align) with what students care about. At several points during the year, students would be asked to identify different goals that currently drive their activities in life (any time frame will do as long as it provides regular, updated information about goals). Leading questions could be:

- Personal goal: What personal quality am I trying to work on?
- Academic goal: What is my current school-related goal?
- Outside life goal: What goal do I have in my life outside of school?
- Future goal: What is one of my goals for the future?

Teachers would enter a shorthand version of each goal in all copies of the grid for that unit and then write a "√" where the lesson and student goal were connected and a "–" where there was no connection. An abundance of minus signs would indicate a disconnect between student goals and what was going on in class, which would be important to address, at least through discussion with the student. A large number of checks could show that the lesson was not only building student knowledge but also helping students to fulfill their personal, academic, life, and future goals. The grid in Figure 6.3 provides only a snapshot of what a few of the case students might look like in an English class during the culmination of a novel unit where students were required to work in groups on a collaborative essay.

While it may not always be possible for a single lesson to relate to all student goals, the simple act of recording when there is a disconnect can help reinterpret behavior that often can be construed as "laziness" or "not wanting to be there." Leaving the explanation with blame centered on the student does not facilitate discussions that account for students' evolving and shifting identities, nor does it lead to any course of action. Although not every problem can be solved, the objective of this grid and any similar recording mechanism is to keep students' goals and lives front and center in the instruction and reflection process. Doing so will recognize that there is often a gap between what students and teachers want students to learn, frequently leading to misunderstandings, restricted participation, and youth efforts to fight back. The goals themselves also can shift the focus onto how young people can develop abilities to expand their available options, freedoms, and relevant future opportunities, even if it is only through casual interactions with teachers and not the lesson itself.

FLEXIBLE IDEAS ABOUT ABILITIES AND INTELLIGENCE

Repositioning young people who too often are stereotyped and stigmatized throughout their school experiences takes much more than a matrix, lesson plan template, and grid. While these tools do not even begin to "fix" the issues students encounter in classrooms, they do represent an effort to mirror the kinds of approaches that can reframe how students with disabilities are perceived. The central message for adults is that information and evidence about students must be constantly collected and updated. The process of gathering this information must reflect the progress and changes students make throughout their lives, both in and out of school. Teacher tools must promote a mindset based on gathering more information, considering how students can develop strengths that meet their goals and needs, figuring out how to expand their available possibilities, and addressing any restrictive environmental barriers.

As earlier cases have illustrated, youth identities are ever-shifting and constantly in motion based on students' experiences across a variety of contexts with people who matter to them in different ways. Repositioning young

FIGURE 6.3. Example of Skill- and Goal-Recording Grid

Time Period: _____   Class: _____

Student Name	Focus Skill #1 Writing essays	Focus Skill #2 Group leadership	Focus Skill #3 Discussion participation	GOALS			
				Personal	Academic	Outside Life	Future
Tinsley	5	1	3	Speak up more √	A in math —	Write book —	Writer √
Mark	4	5	5	Do research √	A on lit paper √	Win debate —	College √
Colby	1	3	3	Lift more weights —	Do math project —	Sing well —	Chef —

people thus requires school-based change, flexible teaching mindsets, and an awareness of the everyday attitudes, messages, and interactions that either confirm or disrupt disabled identities. To make the experience more meaningful, all students and adults must work together to coconstruct a culture conducive to ability development. Even then, interpersonal tensions can threaten to revert to default views about who can succeed. Without intervention and left to their own devices, students can begin competing against one another, teasing or discouraging students who do not fit socially accepted images of success. Parents can further the goal to "be the best" and can promote the desire to compare performance or the goal of fitting in with the "smart" group and being accepted by others. The goals and assessments of the educational system itself can continue to encourage hierarchies that isolate particular students into "lower" groups or "at-risk" categories. Teachers can begin with the most inclusive and supportive intentions, but may not be able to help their anger in the face of defiance and misbehavior or their frustrations in the face of the realities of disappointing standardized test performance. It can be difficult for adults to trust particular students to be able to take on more responsibility for learning, and students can struggle with what to do with their newfound power when the boundaries are too vague. There is a reason why educational reform is cyclical—instituting fundamental cultural changes takes a great deal of monitoring, mediation, and work.

More can be required of young people than simply to be "the best" at fulfilling basic expectations that adults lay out for them. Instead, experiences in the classroom and other learning settings must model and support the kinds of experiences students are already facing and coping with in their everyday lives, including how to deal with failure and challenge (as opposed to merely being the source of experiences with failure). Classrooms can be places where students are supported in coming up with ways they can facilitate their own learning, interact with others in a collaborative way, and position themselves as leaders. In short, how they are treated in the classroom must be as active, flexible, dynamic, responsive, and malleable as their lives demand. Change also cannot be left solely up to adults—young people must be recognized as active participants who can be trusted to lead others under supportive conditions. It is only when learning experiences go unchallenged and negative perceptions remain unchanged that deficit identities "thicken" and forever define who young people are in those places.

Chapter 7

Youth Leadership and Transformative Teams

Miles away from the Music Workshop at Pathways Academy, another 25 students sat in chairs in a circle on the first day of Hillside High summer debate camp in northern California. They looked uncomfortable without the usual protection of the school desks, which were pushed to one side of the classroom. Warily, they eyed one another, as though they wondered what roles they would all play in this unfamiliar environment—who would be the best, who would make them laugh, whom should they avoid? Mark Browning looked overjoyed that there were so many new students, while Anthony Gustafson looked at all the fresh-faced, incoming 9th-graders with an amused expression on his face. And another older student, a 3rd-year named Ana Martinez, looked like she wanted to shrink into the nearest wall. "Hi, I'm Ana," she said when it was her turn during the group "name game" icebreaker. "I'm Ana and I have a sunburn." She pointed at her face with a sheepish expression about the "identifying feature" she chose for everyone to remember. "Hi, I'm Eileen, and I like color!" said a small Asian girl with bangs, large fake yellow plastic glasses, and a bright printed skirt over leggings. Tinsley Hawkins was next, clearly dreading her turn. She looked at her hands and shrugged, saying, "I'm Tinsley, and I'm just . . . Tinsley." As awkward as the experience was, the icebreaker did partially fulfill the promise of its name, for students relaxed their shoulders a bit and started looking around at one another instead of in their laps. At first glance, their faces seemed to portray that they would rather be anyplace else during their summers as they listened to explanations of the 15 different speech and debate events and tried to play it cool. They hid their excitement well. In individual interviews with students at lunch that first day, each of them shyly but enthusiastically described how debate was going to get them into college, win them lots of trophies, or help them become lawyers. Several mentioned how debate was where the "smart kids went," and how their honors English teacher in middle school referred to debate as a way to get into advanced tracks, impress high school teachers, or get good grades. After lunch, the same collection of timid students returned to class, desperate to learn the activity that would ensure them a place in the "smart group" once they entered high school, no matter what their grades were before arriving. Speech and debate equaled success and intellect, particularly given the connection to law and politics. It was only summertime, but in a large, traditional high school such as Hillside, where culture varied with each classroom and instruction was not always in-dividualized, the clock had started and the race to see who could be smartest had already begun.

As McDermott et al. (2006) highlight in "The Cultural Work of Learning Disabilities," changing disabling practices requires a constant battle against deeply embedded "cultural facts." While adults may adjust their mindsets to become more inclusive and ability-oriented, students can continue to rein-force them. The authors continue:

> Even if the teacher manages to treat every child as potentially capable, the chil-dren can hammer each other into negative status positions; and even if both teacher and children can resist dropping everyone into predefined categories, the children's parents can take over, demanding more and more boxes which specify the kinds of kids who do better than others. (p. 15)

In large high schools, incoming students often are left to their own de-vices to carve out a niche for themselves and somehow fulfill the identities they hope to embrace. Those who happen to have the know-how to figure out what activities would gain them the most social capital, or the friends and parents who could connect them with such opportunities, would have a head start in the race for success. The widely held perception that only "advanced" students can participate in debate, for instance, leads to the ex-clusion of students who do not fit this mold, particularly minority students in urban schools or students with varying achievement levels. This chapter focuses on attempts to change perceptions of student capabilities and poten-tial on a debate team, and how students played an active role in transforming these perceptions. The chapter looks at the interaction between teacher-driven inclusive values and youth leadership as the partnership continues to both challenge and reinforce expansive and flexible views of intelligence over time. In doing so, it focuses on the influence of positive social relation-ships, particularly for one case study student, Ana Martinez. The chapter intertwines the discussion with stories from different places in the develop-ment of an inclusive team, in an effort to illustrate how designing, dictating, and planning to reposition youth are only the beginning. Instead, the story of the development of this team continues to explore how one of the most important elements of unlearning disabling practices is for students to be a part of that change. Beyond clearly integrated inclusive cultural values and ability-oriented mindsets, students must be involved as active leaders to make flexible ideas about ability more authentic and meaningful.

In addition to Ana, the illustrations that follow intersect with the stories of the five Hillside case study students (Anthony, Tinsley, Devin, Spencer, and Mark). They also overlap with my own personal experiences and challenges with the Hillside High debate team, as both a researcher and an instructor. Over the course of the study, my role as a researcher was influenced by my job as the founding director and head instructor of the Hillside summer debate institute, working with the same students I studied during the year. As a summer instructor, I had a more direct effect on the team culture. I designed the summer program with the aim of expanding student participation, using multiple instructional strategies and encouraging leadership opportunities, and fostering a community that valued team diversity. Once data collection began during the year, I consciously stepped back from immediate instructional involvement. With that said, an inextricable part of building a group culture is the relationships involved and the interpersonal responsibilities associated with those relationships, which cannot simply be turned off. My relationships with the students on the team, both as an informal mentor and as a source of debate expertise (as a former debater), remained an influence on the cultural development. The cases include the thought process and relational challenges of developing a culture, especially one that privileges the power of youth. While the cases relate to the debate activity, the lessons learned from them are not necessarily unique to debate, suggesting implications for building other transformative group cultures.

ANA AT DEBATE CAMP: "EVERYONE GETS TO TALK"

Ana Martinez sat in the last seat in the back row of morning debate class during the first week of camp, immediately next to her two closest friends, Kelly and Jennifer. Even though she had already been in debate for a year, she was happy to choose the seat in the back, not because she wanted to hide, but because others wanted the front. She sat peacefully, always on time in classy, well-coordinated outfits, with cute shoulder bags containing all the necessary writing utensils and a planner color-coordinated for debate and gymnastics schedules. With her focus maintained on the lesson, she smiled quietly at self-proclaimed "boy-crazy" Kelly, who in turn would burst into giggles at the latest gossip. She took careful notes on speeches that Jennifer would give as one of the first student volunteers, never raising her hand to give a speech herself. When it came time for groupwork, she did volunteer to work with Anthony, who had already established himself as a sort of class clown with his first three entertaining speeches. "Can I see what you wrote? I can't even think right now," said Anthony, leaning over to try to read her neatly hand-written arguments. Ana looked at him skeptically and said, "I don't think you're supposed to write down what I said, but how about you say what you might say back to me?" Without a hint of condescension, Ana continued to prompt Anthony, saying very little except the occasional, "Wait, let me write down what your arguments might be," or "Why do you think that would be true?" Anthony's voice dominated the conversation, but not without subtle, whispered guidance from Ana. She did not even like the Lincoln–Douglas debate and had chosen that "event" only because she had done it before, as the only option the team had before that first summer camp. She found debate scary and never felt prepared, and instead liked events that were both creative and had simple, basic rules. "LD," as it was known, simply had too many unpredictable, spontaneous moments. Even though she rarely spoke and often felt unsure, Ana loved the idea of arguing and imagined standing up in front of everyone and speaking her mind. She was hopeful that the camp eventually could get her to that point. "Debate is like no other class, because you are with people who are smart and you can argue and stand up and say stuff that is important to you," she would say. "And everyone gets to say what they want to say. Like, in a classroom, a teacher will call on certain people, like people who usually talk more, but in this class, everyone gets to talk." It took me until halfway through the 4-week program to hear what she really wanted to say, which shone in the early drafts of her original advocacy on improving art programs for kids. From her confident prose and detailed imagery, one would never know that she recently had been exited from the special education services she had received since elementary school. Instead, her work and hesitant passion silently served as an example to other students, who admired her but did not eat lunch with her. Others went outside while Ana, Kelly, and Jennifer spent the hour lunch in the classroom, with the occasional company of Mark, reminiscing about people in their grade and sharing hopes about junior year.

Broadening Participation and Building the Culture

Teacher-Initiated Change. It was a new cultural transition for Mark and the three girls, who were the only students with any experience before that first Hillside camp. All four students had been part of a small, student-run debate club at the school, where only one debate event (out of 15) was of-fered and students taught themselves. To broaden participation during the summer program and cater to a wider array of learners, I planned a range of debate events to encourage choice, and the instruction itself was built on val-ues of freedom and variation. Students argued in the morning and did spontaneous speaking and acting in the afternoon. They nominated and voted on social activities, and while the 25 incoming 1st years were hesitant about volunteering their opinions at first, they eventually became comfortable with their new role. During the first few lunches, we encouraged students to create student-directed games that involved everyone. The initial weeks of the program also had to reorient students to the idea that freedom and choice actually were encouraged and that not every move had to be dictated. What did need to be dictated was the requirement to applaud and support one another. I was surprised by how much resistance I received to the rule that students had to shake their opponent's hand at the end of a round.

What I also discovered was that, in addition to freedom and choice, the planning and design had to be flexible enough to allow for the organic development of informal learning moments. During the third week, students stopped playing games outside and instead would stay in the classroom at lunch. Beyond the debate instruction, they wanted coaches to tell them "debate war stories" about tournament travel, team friendships, special successes, and trophies won. The "story sessions" were attended by all, and even students who didn't know one another sat in seats, oddly captivated by stories of a world they wanted to enter, oblivious to the warm California sunshine outside. These moments were some of the occasions when I realized that try as I might, mandating that students follow rules for good behavior or even giving them freedom of choice would not automatically make them a team. In some ways the early structures helped provide a basic foundation of cultural expectations to work from, but in other ways they were still artificial. Some students still were not truly respected, and students like Anthony continued to be laughed at despite my protests. Tinsley still escaped to the hallways to sit and text with friends outside the camp, and Ana remained with her same group of friends. Mark positioned himself early on as holding the institutional memory of the team and maintained administrative records, but still was rarely approached by the younger students. Inclusion would not happen overnight, particularly when largely directed by me.

Student-Led Culture. It was not enough for teachers to simply say that every student would have a voice. For this to be the case, students had to actually support one another in what they had to say. While interventions were put in place to make sure that students would be respectful when watching others perform, there needed to be opportunities for everyone to actually be able to demonstrate their strengths and expertise. When Anthony had the chance to display his extensive military knowledge in a way that was deeply relevant to the debate topic, it was easier for students to authentically appreciate what he had to say. When Ana was given the time and structure to prepare a speech on issues she really cared about, her passion shone in her performance, naturally captivating those who listened. The chance to display their strengths was beneficial not only in itself, but also in helping students believe in a broader definition of success. Once they moved away from competing against one another, novice debaters hesitantly started asking experienced debaters for help during independent practice time, prompting some early mentorship opportunities. There was only a certain degree to which teachers could require students to care about one another and trust one another's expertise. It had to be demonstrated by the individual and recognized by the group. It helped to have a final performance night, where students could move beyond their own individual performances and feel like they were part of a broader community. In ways that could not be replicated in training, the high stakes of a performance encouraged students to comfort one another to ease their collective anxiety. Students could see that their voices were valued and feel the support from their peers, families, and broader community. Many were in tears and expressed their deep pride for how far everyone had come. Although they had come a long way during that summer, developing true appreciation for the strengths of others would turn out to be a deeply fragile process—they first had to believe that there was more to success than personal achievement.

HAVING TO STAND: LEARNING THE PRACTICES

The air inside the small, run-down high school cafeteria would have been cold if it had not been for the 50 high school students crammed into it, still wearing suits, disheveled at the end of a long, 7-hour day of competition. As a group, it was only the second tournament for the new Hillside debaters, who were not yet accustomed to the long wait that preceded all speech and debate awards ceremonies. "Come ONNN!!!" complained Devin, eager to hear how he did in his first attempt at impromptu speaking. Ana huddled nervously with Kelly (who was now her acting partner), clutching each other's hands in anticipation. The shine of the trophies was almost too much for the Hillside 1st years, who alternated between sneaking a look at them and burying their heads in the pile of coats and backpacks that littered the table in front of them. Suits borrowed from their parents were already partially shed, leaving suit jackets paired with sweatpants and bunny slippers. One of those pairs of bunny slippers belonged to Eileen, who suddenly squealed, "Hey! It's starting! Ohmigosh, I can't look!" As the awards ceremony began in Devin's event, the announcer quickly scanned through the top seven speakers, which did not include Devin. Once first place was announced, the entire room stood up in a courtesy standing ovation. As I stood automatically, applauding for the first-place winner, I looked over at the Hillside team, only to see that none of them were standing up. "Hey guys!" I hissed quietly. "You have to stand up for first place!" "Why?" whined Devin. "I didn't win anything!" Emma, who was sitting next to him, agreed. "Yeah! It's not like any of us are up there!" As everyone sat down, I hurriedly gathered as many Hillside debaters together as possible without distracting from the continuing awards. "You have to stand up for first place, no matter what. A lot of hard work went into their performance, as you guys know. Even if we don't win, we have to recognize that work." During the next announcement of another first-place winner, Ana and Kelly stood up with me, followed by Eileen and a few other girls. By the final event, half the team was standing, and the challenge of convincing the other half remained.

Competition and Dealing with Disappointment

Teacher-Initiated Change. Promoting a group culture where all students are included and all abilities are appreciated required harnessing the urge to compete with others, which was incredibly difficult to enforce given the nature of the debate activity. Standing for first place, for instance, meant recognizing the abilities and strengths of others, aside from individual performance. Beyond token classroom rules to have students applaud after presentations, students had to be put in authentic, high-stakes situations where they could compete with one another and still appreciate the strengths of the group. In the case of Hillside, every tournament tested students on another level in terms of respecting other people's hard work, even when it meant that they did not always do as well as they wanted. It also tested their ability to deal with failure and resist the negative reactions that competition often would inspire. At tournaments, the coaches went on "walks" with students to debrief rounds and allow them to vent their frustration. This set the precedent that even students like Anthony, who loudly proclaimed that he did not care about winning, or Devin, who quietly stewed over rounds he felt like he should have won, needed recognition of their efforts and support in the face of disappointment.

Student-Led Culture. To create the kind of place where students are comfortable admitting their failures, students had to play a central role in building group unity. To do so, they first had to find a place in the group where they felt like they belonged, and then had to participate in the development of shared practices and experiences. As their first year at Hillside continued, the tournaments gave them a chance to try out many different event options and in the process try on different selves and see what worked. Beginning students like Emma, Eileen, and Natalie did not feel pressured to be stuck in one type of event or face quitting debate altogether. Some of them instead went through five or six events before the first year ended, finally settling on what roles they could feel valued in. Students like Ana could feel confident with others and even feel able to take on leadership roles. Even though she had not won as many tournaments as some of the others, she was elected team president by her peers. I originally had been worried about the team leadership structure, concerned that it might exacerbate stratification on the team in terms of ability and performance or even popularity. This might have been the case if the students on the team had not recognized the value of being led by someone who could mentor and support them, instead of someone who did the best in competition. It is difficult to tell what promoted these values, but if it had been another group of students, the team leadership structure might have gone quite differently. The tournaments themselves gave the students shared experiences that developed into "war stories" of their own, and they shared tales of judge comments, unusual arguments, notable performances, and debate "celebrities" to look out for. Even negative experiences were unifying because they were shared together, such as when the team rallied to defend Devin and Anthony after coach Rebecca Miller discouraged their participation.

Still, to maintain this culture, students continued to need the most support around dealing with disappointment after particular rounds and major losses. Mark would be particularly worried about losing his veteran debater status when 1st-year debaters outperformed him, and other students would be concerned that a loss might threaten their teammates' continued respect for them. While on the surface they appeared to be done competing with one another, the issue was almost that the respect and support they felt from the team could constantly be threatened if they did not perform well. To help one another, some student leaders, including Ana and her friends, started taking one another on walks to talk over disappointments or giving silent hugs whenever a teammate had a bad experience. Students noted this emotional support as fundamentally different from how they were used to experiencing failure in school. Rather than feeling supported by their classmates, students were accustomed to having to face the same kind of anger and disappointment all by themselves, or having to face punitive consequences from parents and teachers for not succeeding. Student-led efforts to help one another with failure represented a departure from the isolationist version of problem solving, and instead encouraged a culture where students could take matters into their own hands and learn how to lead.

REPOSITIONING YOUTH AND LEARNING TO LEAD

The new "interp" acting coach was late again and Ana pulled Jennifer aside in the hallway to brainstorm about what to do. They had a tournament coming up soon and practice could no longer wait for an adult. They had worked well with Jackie in previous practices, but she was a practicing actor and director and often was pulled away for work. With determined expressions on their faces, they gathered the few members of the growing speech squad together and marched off in search of an empty classroom or a teacher who would give them the space. As they were used to doing during independent practice time, they immediately faced the walls and delivered their speeches and practiced their memorization. When that became too uncomfortable, they gathered the desks together and gave collective comments after each person's performance. Hastily thrown together school practices soon became organized sessions at one another's homes, which combined practice with food, gossip, homework, and an occasional movie, blending together productivity and silliness in ways only teenagers can.

Their efforts to coach one another became an official teaching program at the next year's camp, and they were all excited to be chosen for one of the six teaching spots. In the impromptu speaking class, Anthony Gustafson and Natalie Chen calmly prepared for their first solo lesson. Anthony surveyed his class from his perch on the rolling office chair, while Natalie instead had her back to the class, neatly writing out the topic for that day's speech. In his usual, cavalier style, Anthony called the class to attention after lunch. With his hands folded behind his head, he swiveled back and forth, pontificating on the basic rules of impromptu speaking with the ease of a senior partner at a law firm. "I don't think they just want to hear you talk, Anthony," quipped Natalie, in their usual good cop, bad cop routine. "Of course they do! What else would they want to do?" "Maybe they would like to do some actual speaking?" "Oh that! Oh, well, get into two groups or something and then we can get to everyone. And That Means Everyone. Even you, whatever your name is." The two groups looked quite different, as Natalie began organizing her students into set speaker order, setting rules for the audience on how to be respectful, and preparing them with encouraging advice. Each speech progressed in an orderly fashion with a few words of advice from Natalie. In his group, Anthony, who happened to be dressed in a suit that day, immediately started calling on students randomly to give speeches, having them stand in front of the circle because "that's what you'll have to do eventually anyway." When the first speaker finished, all of the new 1st-year eyes swiveled toward Anthony, waiting in awe for what he would say in response. "First off, I really liked how you organized your points and you used your time well . . . at the same time, you paused a lot to think when you should have had already thought it out." Lowering his voice in a conspiratorial tone, he continued, "I remember when I first started impromptu I got up at my first tournament and I was all, UMMM . . . and I didn't know what to say. That doesn't happen forever and it'll get better, don't worry." Each speech was followed by advice and a war story or two, until the clock struck 1:00. As seamlessly as they had taken control, Natalie and Anthony put down the dry erase markers and put away the rolling chair, transforming from teachers back into students.

Emerging Leadership

Teacher-Initiated Change. Students need space to learn how to problem solve and develop the genuine desire to work with one another. Having to figure out how to get more coaching and support forced the students at Hillside to find ways to get additional help because they were united in their desire to improve their performance. At the same time, they needed teacher support in learning how to teach and lead one another. The summer teaching fellows program during the second summer not only aimed to develop those skills, but also was created with the hope of repositioning students as leaders and encouraging active participation. Teaching workshops included a great deal of modeling different strategies they could use, suggestions for how to give critiques and provide more focused feedback, along with concrete planning skills. The classes themselves were cotaught with the coaches for the first few days, followed by a gradual release of responsibility, with students coming up with their own activities, as in Anthony and Natalie's impromptu speaking class. The existence of the program encouraged other students to consider becoming teacher leaders as well, because we promised to show them how. Anthony felt more valued after teaching because other students would listen to him, and his humorous war stories were appreciated instead of shunned. On the other hand, Natalie enjoyed teaching but stopped competing in impromptu because she was afraid of having to maintain a certain level of success to be respected by her students. As she put it, "I don't think I'll ever give an impromptu speech again, especially in front of them. It would be too scary . . . I wouldn't want to disappoint them." Natalie's point again highlights the ever-present fear of failure in the eyes of others and how this can interfere with learning opportunities. When learning to teach and lead others, students also need support for their own performance, both in terms of maintaining their individual skills and in battling fear of what others might think. Leadership opportunities for youth put them in simultaneously valued and vulnerable positions, especially if they are being repositioned in a way that they have never been before.

Student-Led Culture. It would not have been possible to encourage youth leadership at Hillside if the students had not already developed a culture that promoted a vision of success that no longer was built solely on individual student effort. Everyone had a role, and even students who were not coaching oriented were invited by team leaders to come up with team cheers and warm-up activities. While debate certainly could be about individual success, the team set a precedent where focusing solely on oneself was actively discouraged. Other strong role models reached out to younger students, and Ana's leadership modeled the value of helping one another. Younger leaders started mirroring the juniors and seniors, as when Eileen would create team activities and act as a team cheerleader "rallying the troops" to increase energy before rounds. Another student, Kirsten, continued going to tournaments to take pictures and act as team historian, even if she was not competing. Both Eileen and Kirsten were always more than willing to step in whenever the team needed them, such as to substitute for those who were absent at tournaments. Even Mark, who still struggled against the urge to compete against his teammates, switched from a solo debate event to a partner event because he wanted to be part of a team. He was recognized for carrying on the legacy of the team throughout its development by winning the first "Legacy Award," showing how much the team valued the history and traditions of the group. At the same time, whereas culture was being built around team-oriented efforts and student leadership, the pressure of competition threatened to interfere with the emerging inclusive values. The downside of having such a unified peer group was that it increased the students' desire to be accepted in the eyes of their peers, thereby fueling their fear of failure. The value and appreciation they felt from their teammates was something they did not want to lose, and every loss could increase those chances.

BATTLING A FEAR OF FAILURE

The days leading up to tournaments were always nerve-racking, and students gathered in groups around the room with papers strewn all about the desks, with their hair standing on end. Despite their hard work, the computerized tournament entry that Mark would record showed half the numbers on Friday as it did on Monday as more students dropped from tournaments at the last minute. Several students started gravitating toward events with less pressure, or attending practices and approaching coaches with breathless excuses about why they couldn't attend any tournaments that semester. These students still loved the team and spent all of their time hanging out with one another. They still enjoyed the work and put in countless hours practicing speeches and writing cases. And they would say they loved the tournaments the most, but could no longer attend. Somehow, being a sophomore meant that they had to improve, and many worried that they would not pass muster. As a senior, Ana seemed immune to the pressure, keeping her eye focused on her main goal: to qualify for State Championships. But more than that, in the midst of her college applications and endless drafts of her original advocacy speech about not underestimating people with learning disabilities, she continued to mentor others. She was well-acquainted with the fear that was keeping so many of them from doing what they wanted to do. In fact, she wrote about it in her speech and talked about it aloud when easing the worries of her teammates. As Ana stood up for her final round at the state qualifying tournament, she spoke to her audience in a voice that no longer quivered as it had at the first summer camp. "In today's society, whether we are given an official label or not, we still limit ourselves, based on what people think we can or cannot do. For all of us, there are places where we feel disabled. We are all disabled in our own way, but we need to escape these limitations and reach past the labels we put on ourselves and the ones we put on others."

Success vs. Relationships

Teacher-Initiated Change. Escaping the limitations that students put on themselves and on others requires giving students the freedom to seek out new opportunities to redefine themselves. A single moment of failure needs to become just that, a single moment, as opposed to a final judgment that will forever define the future. In the case of Hillside, there were a number of factors that potentially could make perceptions of ability rigid once more. As time went on, some students were not having the success they wanted, and it got harder to always have to be happy for everyone else. Flexible images of success seemed less convincing when the same kinds of kids and same types of performances would always do better than they did. One of the new coaches had a tendency to make fun of students, telling them sarcastically, "You're going to read your speech and if it isn't good enough, I'm going to laugh at you." Sophomores Emma and Kirsten sometimes admitted that they did not feel like they belonged, since they still could not find an event where they fit in and they were getting progressively impatient. Despite efforts to value everyone, certain events were associated with different levels of ability. Events that took more research were positioned as the place where the "smartest" students went, and those that were more creative were perceived as easier or less work. Events based on spontaneous speaking became the place where the "lazy" students went. A new educational hierarchy was born, mirroring similar institutional structures the students were experiencing during the school day. Teachers had to combat this shift by giving students freedom to seek out new opportunities where they could redefine themselves, discover talents they did not know they had, or develop different skills. Two of the new coaches encouraged accessibility by bringing in more partner events, which reinforced the message of valuing unique strengths and collaboration. Continued partner work helped disrupt the hierarchies that were looming once again, where students had to learn to work with one another through teaching experiences and regularly going through the process of mediating working relationships.

Student-Led Culture. When students and teachers alike start to get overly preoccupied with individual performance, they both must work to disrupt the patterns that encourage the obsession with success. There need to be new challenges for students to face, requiring different forms of participation and encouraging collective problem solving. During his 2nd year at Hillside, for instance, Devin found a new event, with the support of Abraham, his new debate partner. As a parliamentary debate team, the two boys were able to build on the different areas of knowledge they each brought to the table, and the impromptu nature of the activity forced them to become more aware of their unique, individual strengths. With his conversational, organized, and clear speaking style, Abraham was the obvious choice for opening and closing speaker, while Devin was valued in the role of the passionate, fiery rebuttal speaker. Together, they reassessed their roles on a regular basis, discussing how they could best capitalize on and "strategize" about what they could each do in the round to win. This partnership was only one of many examples where students proactively sought out roles where they felt their participation would be valued, and were fortunate enough that there were other roles for them to take on.

It was not always easy, but over time students on the Hillside debate team went from a disparate group of competitive overachievers to a true family. In fact, instead of the usual stratified student positions, they began taking on family roles, such as the "mother bears," "fun uncles," "father types," and the new students, like children, would look up to their big brothers and sisters. Instead of being required to respect one another, they actually believed in celebrating their unique strengths. At tournaments, they looked out for one another, planning group activities rather than going off on their own. Like any subculture, they had their own jokes, warm-up routines, traditions, and activities to promote team spirit. They had a common language and could speak to one another with debate lingo that only they could understand. As opposed to their first tournament where they refused to clap for other teams, 2 years later they had "celebrities" from other schools that they admired and could tell stories about. The institutional memory was full of pride in one another, and as new members joined the team, they continued to pass on the team history and traditions, reveling in both the good and the bad. Their experience continues to speak to the importance of shared memories and experiences, and the development of a cultural history of taking pride in the success of others. Truly embracing expansive ideas about intelligence and who can succeed is not something that can be forced—it must be experienced in connection with others.

TRANSFORMATIVE PEER GROUPS

Ana stood calmly in front of the auditorium with the rest of the 13 semifinalists at the state qualifying tournament, while her teammates sat in the audience holding hands and closing their eyes in anticipation. Making it to State Championships was a goal for the entire team, for they had heard stories about the last time they sent students to State Championships, 10 years earlier. But more than that, everyone knew how much the experience meant to Ana. When the results were announced, the entire team stood up for the seven state qualifiers without even thinking, and Eileen, Kirsten, and Emma began to cry when they realized that Ana was one of them. Clutching her trophy, Ana trembled as she walked back over to the team, who all enveloped her in a giant, shaky, tear-streaked hug. "It came true," Ana whispered. "We did it." Although it was Ana who was moving on to represent Hillside, the success was more than hers alone. As she stated at the end of the speech that had qualified her for State Championships, she credited her success to the entire team, who had transformed her from someone who sat in the back row to someone who could realize her dreams. She wrote, "In the small classes and in math class I didn't feel that I was smart enough, and I didn't feel accepted there, I didn't know my strengths. . . . Now I for one may not have felt very smart in math class, but I have experienced my strengths in debate, and I have found a community that appreciates me. In a few months, I will graduate, and I know, as I go out in the world, that there is no limit to what I can do."

Patterns of Cultural Change

Throughout Ana's experience on the debate team, the team's history continually cycled between moments where anyone could lead, bond, and have value, and moments where egos, fear, and disappointment would take over. In the case of the latter, competition would recreate the same stratified, hierarchical divisions that students were used to in other areas of their lives. But through it all, they had a community that they cared enough about to try to make their own, even as they constantly came up against restrictive beliefs about who could succeed. The temptation to reinforce disabling beliefs about others was a challenge faced by both the adults and the students. The process of cultural change took time, continued reinforcement of inclusive values and accessible experiences, and space for the emergence of youth leadership in partnership with adults who were committed to expanding possibilities for everyone. The pressure to win and succeed was often a powerful motivator for students to come together, but at the same time could be the enemy of inclusion. Adults had to set an example by encouraging and supporting a wide range of participants, rather than weeding out (through whatever formal or informal means) students who "looked like" they could not succeed. Students were quite visual and needed to learn by example, especially when they were so used to distinguishing for themselves who was truly valued and why. They needed to see what others were good at, and also needed choices to figure out how to express their own strengths. Over time, the instructors needed to facilitate the process by tailoring and adapting opportunities to help students discover their strengths. There was a constant tension between the urge to revert to more widely held notions of who could succeed in the activity, and constant interventions were required to maintain the inclusive beliefs of the team. Beyond restating expectations for behavior, the environment had to show students how to lead and be flexible enough to be able to take on leadership roles more organically without having to depend on adults. Adults in turn had to show, not only say, that they cared about who students were as people, rather than valuing them only depending on their success.

But adults could not do it alone. Students took advantage of the varied choices and options to take on different versions of themselves, and allowed others to have the chance to be viewed in different ways. They allowed one another to shift and change and experiment without having to fit the same mold of past participation. The experimentation did not go unnoticed and, in fact, they valued those who could demonstrate a wide range of strengths or have unexpected success in a new event. The important shift that students made was to recognize how much they needed one another and how essential it was to act as a team. Together, they battled disruptive, destructive group behavior among themselves, calling one another out on actions that could threaten more open and expansive ideas about who would be able to do well. It helped that they had outside-of-school experiences that showed them how much they needed one another and consistently challenged preconceived notions about who would do well at a tournament. Eileen said it best when she observed, "You really can never predict who is going to do the best. You can work as hard as you can, but that's all you can do." Given the unpredictable nature of success, they still needed the support of adult relationships that could harness and redirect their competitive spirit and help them through disappointment and to have the courage to face failure.

YOUTH REPOSITIONING YOUTH

What made the Hillside debate experience particularly powerful was that leadership and teaching opportunities were used with the express purpose of repositioning young people who often were underestimated by their peers.

While there was teacher-directed support in learning how to teach one another, control was released to students to show off their newfound talents and strengths. The result was that students could appreciate the wide range of capabilities on the team, which were right in front of them—they could see immediately what they could all do because of the constant opportunities to celebrate their strengths. It was a gradual process, but the active roles that all students took in their own debate experience helped unite the team behind a common purpose, and helped the students feel as though there was a goal beyond their personal success. More experienced students were excited when "their novices" received awards, and the younger students felt a sense of pride and awe when they saw other students succeed in events that they had never competed in before. Student-led coaching sessions branched off into student-directed, team-building activities and traditions that felt unique, fun, and special to them. Instead of teachers stepping in as often, students learned to keep one another in check about respect.

As with any culture, though, individual experiences were a product of personal relationships, which were as ever-shifting and dynamic as the individual identities involved. With every new student came a different challenge to maintaining the idea that all students could be appreciated for their strengths and abilities. The picture was never as neat as it may have seemed on the surface, especially in an activity as intellectually competitive as debate. Both students and adults could fall victim to ideas that some students were not "good enough" or "well-suited" to certain events, or even to the debate activity itself. Adults and students needed one another to help challenge deficit-oriented mindsets and figure out new ways to appreciate the strengths of the whole team. The variety of events, flexibility involved in choices for learning, and tournament experiences offered a unique setting for helping all students explore their abilities—but this kind of culture does not have to be exclusive to debate. The important lesson was the need for youth-driven transformation: For the process to be authentic, meaningful, and lasting, young people had to play a central role in repositioning one another. Whether in a classroom or on a team, young people need a place that fosters active involvement and where positive interpersonal relationships are both possible and powerful. In addition to challenging rigid notions of success, encouraging youth leadership allows adults to get to know young people in a more profound way and gain a stronger grasp of their identities in ways that can be quite surprising. The more that both adults and youth can be open to those surprises, the more they can be open to challenging assumptions, and the more likely disabling practices are to change.

Fly–Fight–Win

The school version of Anthony did not change much over the years, and he still sat slumped in his chair, reading a book from home or chattering to a nearby student about video games. The more proactive teachers told him to be quiet because he talked too much, and his powerful voice and goofy jokes often would steal the spotlight from the lesson at hand. At times, these interactions would become heated and Anthony, who never took kindly to confrontation from teachers, would say, "If you yell at me, I'm going to yell back at you, and you know who will win that war." The more passive teachers let him read independently so they wouldn't have to deal with him, even if it meant he was behind on the material. There were good days and bad days, and geometry was the constant battle. Even good days seemed like a celebration merely because nothing negative had happened, and it always felt like everyone was holding their breath, waiting for him to disrupt the class with a joke or two. People liked him, but few took him seriously. It all seemed confusing and foreign, because we saw nothing of the polished, driven young man we were getting to know. It was even difficult to talk to him during school. I often felt like a parent, taking care not to be an embarrassment, keeping a careful distance in the hallway, and only giving the occasional, noncommittal nod of acknowledgment before continuing on my way. Real interactions and windows into his hopes for the future in the military were reserved for debate tournaments and family shooting trips.

I had been excited at first when Anthony invited us all to go to the shooting range with his family, especially since I had heard so many dinnertime stories of their connections to the military and law enforcement. While busy schedules prevented them from going to the shooting range as often as they'd like, it was an activity they enjoyed together to relax on weekends. I knew it would be an important piece of the Anthony puzzle for me to witness as part of the study. To say the least, this would be different from our other home visits. Once my academic motives for the outing gave way to the realization of what we actually were going to do, my heart beat a little faster. Maybe I could just watch, I thought, already forming my excuses around needing to film or take photos and notes. As the car rolled across the gravel road leading up to a small wooden building, I could see Anthony and his dad standing by their truck, ready for the arrival of my family in Greta's white station wagon. Before my mom, sister, husband, and I were completely out of the car, Anthony Sr. began giving instructions and handing out earplugs. "Please listen carefully. When we go out there, there will be a buzzer and you must put down your firearm and point it down-range and step away behind the yellow line. At that point in time, we will be able to go and look at our targets, but it is very important that you follow the instructions they will give you over the intercom. They are very strict about that here and safety is of the utmost importance. Put in your earplugs and twist them so they go in and expand to deaden the noise." With that, we all followed behind him as my sister and I shared a nervous glance. There was no backing out now.

Anthony and his dad were wearing matching camouflage jackets, and there was a sense of professionalism about Anthony as he waited for his father's instructions that was different from anything I had witnessed before. They moved in unison, and when he did not have a specific task to set up, Anthony stood off to the side, his hands folded in front of him and his feet shoulder-width apart, like a soldier at ease. As Anthony Sr. led us into the main office, Anthony carried rifles from the truck over to a long row of benches covered by a wooden overhang looking out to the targets 25 yards away. We signed up and followed single file past the bearded men shooting their handguns; there was not a single woman in sight other than Greta, who was only a spectator. One of my earplugs slipped and the sound from a nearby Glock was startling. Greta and the rest of us stood off to the side and let the Anthonys take over our station, setting up the firearms and hanging targets. Anthony introduced us to the three rifles, including a new M-16 named "LaShonda."

My mind wandered as they finished their preparation. I couldn't help but smile at the memory of my initial doubts about Anthony's dad really being in the Coast Guard Special Forces or his mom being former Air Force. While we stood there, waiting for them to give us instructions, all of my assumptions that Anthony had been exaggerating in his stories seemed very far away. In fact, his dad seemed more at home in his camouflage jacket than in casual street clothes. Well into the second year of the study, it was striking to finally see them in action together. Considering that we had heard so many stories about Anthony's interest in the military, we had limited chances to see it in context. During our home visits, I observed Anthony's lengthy sessions on his computer, researching different careers in the military and looking up possible positions he might be interested in. At the dinner table, his dad shared stories of combat while Anthony listened intently. Although he was in several after-school programs, due to the nature of Young Marines, it was difficult for us to observe his participation and we did not want to make him uncomfortable in any way. We were able to attend Anthony's award ceremony for his police shadowing program, however, where we saw him accept his leadership award wearing his police cadet uniform. I also saw a glimmer of his training when I had to leave a debate tournament to go to the emergency room with a concussion a few months before. Together with one of the coaches, Anthony exhibited speed, efficiency, and professionalism I had never seen before and was incredibly grateful to have. But despite the hints at his other life, this was our first taste of how much more than a hobby this was to them. A simple outing for target practice or not, this was serious business and we were lucky to be invited.

"Ah! There's nothing like the smell of gunpowder in the morning, is there?" Although he was focused and careful with the preparations, Anthony was noticeably relaxed. I took his cue to remind myself to breathe and notice my surroundings. The air smelled of smoke and recent rain, and the morning sun was beginning to emerge from behind grey clouds. Despite the muffled booming sounds and my own anxiety, I could not help but notice how peaceful it was. Anthony smiled to himself and bent over to examine the scope of the middle rifle, a British-made Bolt rifle that he previously had described in great detail. He was interrupted by a bell signaling that it was okay to load guns and begin our session. "Who wants to go first?" Anthony Sr. looked around at our blank faces, as we felt like students trying to avoid being called on by the teacher. After my sister and husband went a few rounds and examined their targets, it was my turn. I put down the Flip camera and joined Anthony Sr., who picked up the oldest rifle, which Anthony had first learned on. He instructed me in how to hold and aim the rifle as well as how to load the ammunition. He stood back to watch as I awkwardly positioned it. The first few rounds didn't go too badly, and when we went to examine our targets, Anthony congratulated me on my progress and then provided me with additional pointers and a teaching session on how to use LaShonda.

"Now, when you hold LaShonda, you have to make sure you bring the gun to you, don't go to the gun. Also, make sure your hand is wrapped around it right there . . . not too low . . . that's right. Rest it on your shoulder and lean your cheek on it lightly, don't press it there . . . that's what my mom does. You got it, now, it will look a little different when you aim it, but it's pretty much the same idea as before. Are you going to try it sitting down or standing up? If you're standing up, watch your stance, it should look like this." As I made my first attempts with LaShonda, Anthony stood back and watched my progress, becoming the teacher and giving me a few reminders on my technique along the way. I was not accustomed to such a role reversal, but as I took my unsteady steps into his world, I could appreciate his expertise and comfort level to a greater degree than I would simply from behind the lens of a video camera.

"Isn't this such a stress reliever?" said Anthony Sr., smiling for the first time. "It takes a little while to get it, but it's so satisfying to see the middle of your target turn clear." By that point, we had been shooting for an hour, and my family stood back to let the Gustafson family take the next round. Once the bell rang, the three of them quietly took up their firearms and shot with what looked like perfect technique to my untrained eye. Unlike when we tried, there was no giggling or talking, and they each seemed to be in their own little world. I would never have described a shooting range as a peaceful place or Anthony as a peaceful person, but somehow, on that morning, this was peace.

A few months later, at a debate tournament, Anthony and I sat outside between rounds chatting about that morning at the shooting range and his military goals. It was late January and it had just rained, so we stood as we spoke, with light misty rain smearing the ink on the open page of my notebook. "I know the military is really important to you, especially the Air Force . . . 'Fly–Fight–Win,' right? That's their motto? I want to write about it, but I need you to help me understand more about it. I have a lot of notes on things you've talked about before, but it's hard for me to put it altogether."

Anthony cut me off, eager to educate me. "Well, when I was 16 and a half, I called up a recruiter who I had talked with before. Usually they don't like talking too in-depth with kids that young, but she remembered that I was really motivated and serious about it unlike some other people, and I had really good parent support. I had met them when I was a freshman when they visited the school. I saw them again when I went to the mall and decided to go into the office because I happened to be there. I just took the ASVAB a few weeks ago, which is like the SAT for the military, and got an 81 out of 99, which means I am basically qualified for any job. It would be great to be a bomb technician, but my dad doesn't really want that. I'll probably be an apprentice and haul equipment and do security, but one of my goals is to call airstrikes and be in the JTAC special ops and one-up my dad. You need good leadership skills for that."

I smiled at that because few people at the school would have considered him to be a leader. He was very private about the leadership award he won, except for when he shyly brought his plaque into debate class and showed it to a few of the girls during the second summer program. He did not tell his teachers. For someone normally so gregarious, he was remarkably private about recognition or opportunities to pursue leadership. I remembered how shortly after Anthony won the trophy at the novice tournament, we were sitting in a parking lot in his mom's car on the way to a home visit. His mom had forgotten something at work and Anthony waited until she had gotten out of the car and slammed the door before asking, "You know how you were talking about having some students apply to help you teach at the summer program this year? Do you think I could be one of those teachers?" I had hoped Anthony might apply to my first annual teaching fellow program, but I didn't know whether it would occur to him. I agreed, and as soon as his mom re-entered the car, the discussion was over. He was a fantastic student leader that summer, and he took pleasure in nonchalantly announcing to family and friends that he couldn't hang out with them too late, that he had a job and had to get up early. The same voice that had proved so problematic in other classes was an asset to him in debate class, and while he still told jokes, he also provided advice to the younger students as they hung on every word.

"I'm going to get my medical and physical next month and I will finally take my oath of enlistment," Anthony was saying as I jerked my thoughts back to the current conversation. "Then, I will go to basic training for 8 weeks and a really intense 1-week 'make it or break it' training. Then I'll have 2 weeks of hometown recruiting by the end of next year. I really want to be stationed somewhere in New York or in the airborne command, para-trooping. I still have to wait until I turn 18, but hopefully if everything goes okay, I'll finish basic training and be stationed in Afghanistan by the end of 2012. I'll get to eventually retire in the year 2031." As he described all of the required steps, he spoke deliberately and confidently, as though there was no doubt about his future path. I was almost jealous of how sure he was about life and how detailed his plan was. Undoubtedly it would shift with time, but it was still a plan, which was more than I could always say for myself.

As I scribbled down notes, Anthony's voice became softer and more serious, and without pausing, continued, "I actually sat down with my parents and discussed the life insurance plan they should take out, you know, if I die. I want the money to go to a scholarship in my name for a student to go to art school. I want it to be a high-need student who doesn't have all the things I've had in life. I want to be remembered for something peaceful, not violent, and I always wished I could be an artist. I don't have the talent for it, but if I were to come back in another life, I would want to be an artist. I want to be buried at Arlington, and I want my funeral to have a lot of alcohol and for people to have fun and not be sad. I'm not being morbid, it's just something that might happen, you know? I hope it won't, of course, but I want to be remembered as someone fun, for something peaceful."

I didn't know what to say, and at that moment one of the other debaters ran up to us and gestured eagerly to Anthony, pointing at a go-cart that had been left a few feet away from where we were standing. "I can't believe they left that there," said Anthony, with a devilish glint in his eye. "And look! They left the key in the ignition! That is waaay too tempting, why would you do that with all of these high school students around? I almost wish they hadn't left the key, I've always wanted to learn how to hotwire a car." The two boys ran off, making their plots but not acting on them, letting their imaginations run wild with images of themselves joyriding around the campus, leaving me with a new appreciation of Anthony's future path.

Unlearning Disability

The past is never dead. It's not even past.

—William Faulkner, *Requiem for a Nun,* 1950

Under the shadow of painful personal histories, young people continue to keep an eye on the future and fight forces that tell them they will never achieve what they set out to do. Their experiences ebb and flow, and they encounter spaces that constrain what they can do as well as people who show them how they can resist those constraints. For as many positive, inclusive changes that can occur in any learning setting or in larger systemic reform, disabling social forces always lie in wait, threatening to reinforce social hierarchies. As Faulkner says in the quote above, people carry the past with them, and while negative school experiences do not always have dire life consequences, they can have an unexpected impact on how people view themselves and what they see as possible. Even in casual conversations, too many people can tell stories that mirror the ones told in this book. When I tell the tales from these chapters, it does not seem to matter whether someone has a disability or not—people can quote, in detail, their own moments when teachers would tell them that they weren't "smart," that they would "never be good at math," or that school would never be "their thing." Like Anthony, they had to change schools too many times or felt depressed early on about their classroom experiences. They were afraid to share their talents in school because they believed they would not be welcomed, as Tinsley so often felt. They may have felt discriminated against because of what they looked like or mistakes they made in the past, such as with Devin and Spencer. Frustration and bitterness were common emotions; like James, they never thought their intelligence was appreciated in school or, like Mark, they constantly felt caught up in a desperate race to succeed. Even when school was generally a positive experience, as it was for Colby and Ana, the stress about meeting expectations and pleasing others could challenge even the most resilient of personalities.

While each of these cases is unique, they are indicative of the larger problem underlying social disablement. Subjective external forces such as institutionalized discrimination and bias continue to influence who is considered "smart" or "intelligent," restricting participation and scopes of possibilities. The stories told here exemplify how, in the face of such restrictions, young people need to expand their available possibilities by developing abilities that give them more control over their lives. Unfortunately, stereotypes based on past behavior, race, gender, class, disability, and other markers of identity "put a threat in the air" and restrict access to valued opportunities to develop those abilities. Students continue to face ongoing contradictions between how they imagine themselves and their future lives, and the concerns of teachers, schools, and other influential figures, which can contribute to deficit academic identities. To resolve these contradictions and exercise their agency, young people resist disabling practices in a number of ways, including fighting to prove their worth, creating outside spaces in which to develop passions, and rejecting academic values. While their efforts demonstrate how young people are not powerless in the midst of disabling practices, they cannot be left unsupported in doing so. The power to support and reposition youth lies in the creation of flexible, supportive school-based structures and the promotion of ability-oriented mindsets for teaching based on gathering more information about student identities. Most important, the power to reposition youth lies within the young people themselves, if we help them promote cultural change through meaningful, authentic relationships that value the strengths of all people.

There is no easy, single action or cultural shift that can permanently expand scopes of possibilities for all children. Even where efforts seem to succeed, they easily can crumble under the pressure and temptation to figure out who is "the best." Instead, a more fruitful discussion regarding educational change must examine the environmental barriers that young people face. Rather than asking what is wrong with individual students or teachers, the question must break down the subliminal social messages that tell some students that their dreams will never be possible. Criticizing environmental features does not absolve people of the role that everyone plays in perpetuating disabling practices. It is tempting in such discussions to cross the line into purely intellectual, theoretical, and academic debates that actually move away from the stories that inspired them in the first place. The key to change lies in being aware of everyday experiences with disablement, promoting practices informed by concrete information about students' lives and histories, and recognizing that mindsets and assumptions about learning influence how young people are treated. It will not be possible to unlearn disabling practices if there is too little understanding of what they are, what they look like, and what they can do to students' lives. Stories of ongoing pain, hardship, and borderline abuse go unrecognized (or even worse, taken for granted) too often in an educational system that still wonders what is wrong with its students. Learning theories are disregarded by practitioners as the web of abstractions they frequently are, instead of as a way to make perceptions, assumptions, and values more visible and understand their effects on practice. True cultural change requires a shift in those values and assumptions, which must involve all people, including the youth whose lives they impact most.

The problems are deep and far-reaching, but change is not impossible. Some of the smallest, seemingly inconsequential moments have changed students' lives forever, in ways they will never forget. Colby will always remember how LaShonda told him that he was a performer and how his teachers told him they believed he had the courage to be himself. Ana will forever hold her peers on the Hillside debate team responsible for supporting her in finding her voice. Mark still remembers how his special education teacher taught him ways to display his intellect, the trips his parents would plan to encourage his interest in history, and the winning debate rounds that allowed him to prove himself. James was grateful for the opportunity to go on nature trips and still believes he can pursue science, even if teachers doubted his ability. Spencer could always turn to his debate coach, who encouraged his argumentative tendencies while also making sure he ate. Devin still remembers our interaction at his first debate tournament, where he learned not only the skills to improve his debating ability but also how to teach others. At home, Tinsley never took her mother's support for granted, for she gave Tinsley the space to write and create her own imaginary world. And Anthony will always be grateful for the family members, instructors, and team members who saw something else in him besides the disruptive class clown he so often was assumed to be. Such tales demonstrate how, despite the systemic and societal nature of disabling practices, change is always possible in the everyday interactions and relationships built with young people. Being a supportive presence in the midst of disablement, and communicating the desire to expand possibilities for all young people can be powerful to students who feel alone in resolving contradictions, pushing back, and creating opportunities for themselves. Promoting the flexible structures, universal mindsets, and youth leadership opportunities to challenge the cultural status quo are moves of change that are within the power and ability of all of us to make possible, no matter how entrenched these practices might be.

Epilogue

As Anthony bent his head over the pages of the dissertation this book was based on, I could catch only an occasional smile followed by an amused chuckle. I was nervous about sharing my account with him and could only hope I was able to appropriately capture these small moments in his life. He read the first part quickly, slowing down during "Fly–Fight–Win." He neatly stacked the pages together and handed them back to me, not looking me in the eye. As soon as I had them in my hands, he asked, "Can I see that last one again?" For the next 5 minutes, he slowly read over the passage. "Can I keep this? Is this your only copy?" "Sure, you can keep it." "It's just that I don't have much that records the things that really mean a lot to me. When I enlist, I want something to help people understand how I really feel about it." I nodded, flattered that what I had written meant so much to him.

"You know, it's funny seeing it all from your perspective, I mean, I remember all of it happening, but it's funny to see how you saw it. That interview with my mom . . . that really brought back a lot of memories from some of the worst times in my life." "Well, hopefully . . . did I get it all correct?" "It's not exactly a pysch report, it's kind of like . . . Hemingway! I had no idea my life was that interesting!"

We continued our conversation, both amused about how this entire story unfolded and reflecting on some of the memories described. When I first met Anthony, I could never have predicted what it would be like to enter his world. It is one thing to theorize about how identities develop, and it is another thing completely to have my life changed through my adventures with Anthony. I am still embarrassed to think that I ever questioned whether his stories were true, or that I doubted whether he would be able to go to a debate tournament and give a speech without goofing off. He completely changed my thoughts on choosing the military over college and taught me about the importance of choosing a path that is right for the individual. When I see him at school and people who barely know him make generalizations about his future, I feel offended at first. Then I remember that I probably would do the same thing if I had not witnessed his incredibly rich, complex story. It is easy to make assumptions about people.

A year after the data collection had ended and my dissertation was long defended, I found myself standing in Anthony's backyard amid my family, his relatives, a few teachers, and the Hillside debate team, all of whom he had invited for their involvement in helping him "achieve important milestones." It was his going-away party before beginning his Air Force training, and there was an air of sadness to Anthony's exchanges as he politely greeted each of his guests. After the "patriotic picnic"–themed buffet, and after I had chatted with all of the people I had gotten to know because of Anthony, he gathered everyone into a circle. One by one, he recounted stories about how each person had changed him and made a difference in his life. In true Anthony form, he occasionally broke the mood with an unfortunate joke or two, but the sentiment was clear: A new chapter was finally beginning with the help of those he loved.

Due to the interconnected nature of the social networking world, this would not be the last anyone would hear from Anthony. While we could keep up with his latest complaints about the physical toll of his new life, he also kept up with his debate team. On Thanksgiving, he posted the following message:

> Today I'm thankful for all the coaches and my teammates for supporting me during my time at Hillside High. The team felt like one big family. I know I couldn't have made it without y'all's support. . . . I keep seeing how well y'all are doing and it makes me so proud to think I was once part of the team. I miss you guys and I'm so proud of you. Congratulations and keep up the good work.

His post was greeted by an outpouring of love from teammates who felt the same way. As debate tournaments continued, the phrase, "Remember when Anthony . . . " often was interspersed in stories about fun they had on the team. There were regular references to speeches he had given or quotes from jokes he had told. And whenever the team wished they could interact more with other schools, someone would always say, "I wish Anthony were here. He'd know what to do."

Every experience changes who people are as individuals, as friends, as students, as children, and how they engage in each role they play. There may be many positioning attempts to force a person into boxes to save time and effort in making sense of who they are, but human identities don't work that way. Making sense of identities requires a great deal of questioning, supporting one another's quests for answers, and living life together through all the confusion. Similarly, although I have reached the end of this particular installment, there are so many questions left unanswered. How could I ever look at a student again without feeling woefully uninformed about his or her life? If there's one lesson I learned from Anthony, it is that there is no harm in asking, and hopefully next time I will be lucky enough again to be welcomed in.

Ability Across Contexts: Methods and Realities

In his book *Long Engagements: Maturity in Modern Japan*, David Plath (1980) argues that human growth is always shaped by culture and society, a "mutual building of biographies, a collective shaping and self-shaping of lives according to a heritage of values" (p. 5). He writes:

> Culture, character, and consociates weave a complicated fabric of biography. The process is not only lifelong; it is longer than we are born, and may continue to renegotiate the meaning of our life long after we are dead. To this extent, a person is a collective product. We all must "author" our own biographies, using the idioms of our heritage, but our biographies must be "authorized" by those who live them with us. (p. 9)

As I attempted to understand individual stories, I soon discovered it would be impossible for me to do so without examining how my own subjective biography was intertwined with the people in my study. Despite my many attempts to distance myself as an ethnographer, I often had to rely on my interpretations of other people's perspectives. Wolcott (1997) notes that "the ethnographer walks a fine line. With too much distance and perspective, one is labeled aloof, remote, insensitive, superficial; with too much familiarity, empathy, or identification, one is suspected of having 'gone native'" (p. 331). Harold C. Conklin insists good researchers "must respect the phenomena [they] describe" (Kuipers & McDermott, 2007, p. 3). Even though I came to the research with certain theories and a developing intellectual identity, I had to keep my eyes open to what was happening around me. Given that ethnography necessitates the long-term engagement of the researcher (Walford, 2008), I was a continuous witness to the change and growth of the participants. To represent these perspectives fairly, I had to remind myself constantly to be open to change and growth myself.

When I began this study, I thought I would be describing the everyday experiences of these young people, attempting to construct biographies that would adequately represent who they were and what they cared about. What

I neglected to realize until later was how I was also a continuous part of their lives, and that their stories were also my story. While I entered this study with a foundational understanding of identity and positioning literature and a sense of the phenomena I wanted to observe, my beliefs were constantly evolving as a direct result of the young people I encountered. This process was almost more important than the final product because it revealed how building relationships with young people can guide and shape a framework that is grounded in their actual lives.

Why Ethnography?

While ethnography is not a typical methodological approach for studies of people with disabilities, I found this method to be appropriate given my focus on how these individuals formulate identities by moving within different social worlds. To understand how my case study students took part in cultural practices in a community (Geertz, 1973), I needed to consider the "everyday detail of individual lives with wider social structures" (Walford, 2008, p. 7). Through an ethnography, I hoped to understand the nuances of their experiences by collecting a diverse range of data, taking an active, continuous role in their lives over time, engaging in a constant process of theory building, and highlighting the voices of participants above the power of the researcher (Madison, 2005; Walford, 2008; Willis & Trondman, 2000). These methods do not aim merely to report events that happen to people, but aim to help make sense of cultural practice. Geertz (1973) continues, "The claim to attention of an ethnographic account does not rest on its author's ability to capture primitive facts in faraway places and carry them home like a mask or carving, but on the degree to which he is able to clarify what goes on in such places, to reduce the puzzlement" (p. 16). In my case, the puzzlement extended beyond the cases to my own understanding of how students were experiencing their lives across different contexts.

Identifying "Disability"

One of the major challenges in the field was how to simultaneously recognize that, while "disability" could be a social construct with more complex links to identity, I would need a more concrete way of identifying students who "had disabilities" in order to study them. In the end, I designed an informational survey that would provide me with initial information about their interests and out-of-school lives along with information about disability. Given how differently people identify with "disability," one of the survey questions asked students about whether they had ever had an IEP, 504 Plan, speech therapy, individualized instruction, or any other kind of accommodation. Their responses helped narrow down the group of students, since these factors tend to indicate a "disability" label. I also wanted to choose students whose families would be supportive of the study, especially over 2 years. Finally, I chose students who immediately stood out from the crowd, not only because of their disability label, but because of what I noticed from their class participation. They included not only students who stood out because they were loud and argumentative but students who seemed to withdraw from the crowd. In the end, I chose nine students, eight of whom are described in this book, which seemed like an appropriate number given the amount of time the fieldworkers and I could spend in each context over the 2 years.

Important Ethnographic Elements and Realities

While each ethnographic study requires a different methodological approach, the subjective nature of this work necessitated a combination of multiple research tools, including a constant re-evaluation of ethnographic theory, method, and technique. As Conklin (1964) writes:

> In such an ethnography, the emphasis is placed on the interpretation, evaluation, and selection of alternative statements about a particular set of cultural activities within a given range of social contexts. This in turn leads to the critical examination of intracultural relations and ethnotheoretical models . . . Demonstrable intracultural validity for statements of covert and abstracted relationships is a primary goal. (p. 25)

To collect data on the cases in this book, I incorporated the following elements of ethnographic work: theory building, data collection methods based in participant observation, attention to participant–researcher relations, simultaneous analysis and evaluation of the theoretical framework, and careful, "thick description" (Geertz, 1973) during the writing process. To ensure that I was being rigorous with my study methods, I used multiple tools of data collection and interpretation. These included interviews with the students, families, teachers, administrators, and friends; extremely enlightening home visits; classroom and program observations; and looking at student work. To facilitate this process, I videotaped and audiotaped my interactions with students, resulting in over 2,000 hours of recorded data beyond the written fieldnotes. Throughout the 2-year process, my theoretical framework and research questions evolved as I listened to participants' accounts. This continuous framing focused on relevant ways of clarifying patterns that emerged from the data, rather than "abstract, grand theory" presented for the sake of theory alone (Madison, 2005; Willis & Trondman, 2000).

Data were collected by three other researchers as well as myself—a team of four people, one devoted to each school, while I supervised all three contexts. While one of the people collecting data was not involved in educational research, two were fellow doctoral students working on their own dissertations. To work successfully as a team, we had to define our research goals from the beginning, decide on an organizational structure that worked for all of us, and create a system for debriefing and sharing fieldnotes (Erickson & Stull, 1998).

Because we were in three contrasting high schools in two states in addition to a wide range of activity contexts, we developed different relationships with the participants. In the debate team setting, I found that my past experience as a debater encouraged "inclusive overtures" (Emerson & Pollner, 2001), where people tried to see me as a resource or a member of their community. When compared with the other two settings (one in which I often was invited to act as a member of the group and the other where I remained a fairly passive observer), I often felt as though I was managing three separate ethnographies. Rather than having the study conform to the neat structure I had planned, these varying relationships influenced the type of data I could collect and amount of access I had to different contexts. My relationships with everyone we encountered thus helped shape my impressions of them, my interpretations of their everyday experiences, the research questions themselves, and ultimately my conceptualization of ability and identity.

While it might seem intuitive that contexts are dynamic and complex, I struggled against this concept for my first few months in the field. My early observation and interview guides even divided up my notes and questions in terms of relationships, opportunities, culture, and expertise, with a separate section for describing the context. My notes on the first participant interviews did not capture the spirit of the individual responses that emerged so clearly when I listened to them months later. The first day in each context, the majority of my fieldnotes fell into either the "relationships" or "context" columns. I quickly abandoned the process of putting observations into thematic categories before actually doing any observations, something that I should not have been doing in the first place (Emerson, Fretz, & Shaw, 1995).

When I first entered the three programs, my premature analysis made it difficult to handle just how different each of the contexts were from one another because I had pulled apart what social features I wanted to look at before I had a real sense of their relational qualities. While I knew their differences on paper (different subject matter, different schools, and different goals), and was aware this would have an impact on "identity," I had not appreciated the complexity. Every context brought a whole new set of thoughts and questions with regard to my framework, and it appeared as though I would have to create three completely different models of identity. Reluctantly, I eventually had to set aside the theory for the time being, immerse myself in each context, and simply listen to the voices of the people in front of me.

Gaining Entry in the Field

For the first 4 months of the study, I observed students only in their program settings, which included the Hillside High debate team, Pathways Music Workshop, and an ecology class at Jefferson. To this day, I consider myself lucky that I ended up in contact with interested, encouraging adults in each program, who helped me gain access to these settings and other contexts important to my case study students. At Pathways, I initially contacted Bill Wright, who was in charge of the innovative partnership between professionals and students known as the Music Workshop. Although Bill had no background in music himself, when he retired he got in contact with LaShonda Evans, who had been a solo performing artist in Las Vegas. Together, they worked on building a partnership between music performers and Pathways Academy, encouraging students to perform and write songs. Both Bill and LaShonda were immediately welcoming and facilitated my early data collection by setting up an area for filming, contacting us about performances, and providing us with copious background information about each of the students, the school, and the history of the program.

Gaining access to the partnership between the University of Washington and local high schools in the Pacific Northwest was a completely different experience. I initially spoke to the program manager at the University to find out more about the partnership, where graduate students in the School of Oceanography paired with classroom teachers to teach, communicate research, and work with high school students. She invited me to speak to the scientists and teachers at an end-of-year informational workshop to garner interest in the study. Unlike the one-on-one interview with Bill at Pathways, my presentation for this group was greeted with both interest and skepticism. Rather than asking for more details about the study, the scientists immediately questioned my ethnographic research design, demanding that more quantitative measures be included (a common critique of ethnography). After an hour-long drilling session dominated largely by the scientists instead of the teachers, the group broke for lunch, giving me time to talk to people individually. Julie Simms, a high school ecology teacher at Jefferson High, approached me with a sympathetic expression, saying, "I don't think I heard one question about kids out of any of them! Why are they so obsessed with numbers? I love what you're doing—would you like to come observe my classes?" I spent the rest of the lunch hour discussing the project with Julie and her graduate student partner, Alex, who had been one of the few scientists to ask about the complexity of disability labels. Over the summer, we made plans for me to make a few exploratory visits to their classes to identify a setting to observe.

That same summer, I was also in the process of developing a pilot study in California to help me practice and explore some of the methods I would use in the ethnography (particularly using audio and video equipment). This pilot study focused on the social experiences of students with disabilities in a summer debate institute that I founded and directed. In addition to my personal familiarity with this school (having grown up in the area), I was able to gain access to it as a research site through Hillside's principal, David Sanchez, and special education teacher Mike Fitzgerald. Mike had been serving as the debate teacher for 3 years, but was concerned about getting more students interested and enrolled to keep the program alive. Having been a debate coach, I offered to create a summer institute, which ended up recruiting 25 new students to the team. Eighteen of these students consented to be part of the pilot study, which included four individual interviews each, and audio- and video-recorded participant observation during debate classes. Since I was teaching for part of the day, I sought the help of an undergraduate student, Aurora, who ended up as part of the research team for the ethnography.

As I transitioned from the pilot study to the larger ethnography, I was often grateful for the opportunity to build trusting relationships with the students over the summer as well as with Mike, the debate parents, and Principal Sanchez. These relationships made it much easier in terms of access to the site, choosing participants, collaborating with and trusting another researcher to collect data while I was in other sites, and overall methodology. This was particularly valuable given that I was based in the Pacific Northwest during the school year, with only monthly visits to California. The hardest part about conducting this pilot study was my transitioning from an instructor role during the summer to an ethnographer role during the school year. Since I had built up a certain rapport with the students as a coach, it was difficult to respond when students asked for my help with their work or when they had problems with another adult. While I made sure to take a backseat in many of these conflicts, there were times when I felt it was most ethical to intervene to support them and fulfill an obligation to my participants. These decisions and my reasoning for them were recorded in detail in my fieldnotes.

Role of the Researcher and Addressing Subjectivity

From the beginning, it was easy to see that these three settings were incredibly different from one another, not only because of the living contexts themselves but also because of the students who were involved. While I started with a clear list of what types of data to collect, when to collect them, and what contexts I wanted to observe, I had to adapt to different situations and make instinctive decisions about what was appropriate. It was also inevitable that the more time I spent with the students, the more I wanted to advocate for them or intervene on their behalf. Not only was my own personal history a mediating factor in how I understood what was happening in front of me, but by spending so much time with the students, I was truly brought into their world. While this can be considered a good thing in terms of building strong relationships with participants and allowing them to trust us, my subjectivity undoubtedly influenced what kinds of data I collected, how I interpreted those data, and what kinds of questions we asked. All of these things are necessary when dealing with the daily, lived experiences of real people, but it was important to maintain a balance between distance and involvement.

I could not deny my own subjectivity as well as the subjectivity of the contexts themselves, for research is deeply influenced by the nature of human interaction. I followed advice from Lareau (1996) for maintaining methodological integrity, with steps such as talking to colleagues to develop questions, having written interpretations critically reviewed by others, and regularly comparing findings with the existing literature. It helped to communicate with the team and compare interpretations of situations, especially since we all had days when we observed together as well as days observing on our own. Beyond the research team, all data also were critiqued during informal presentations at the LIFE Center at the University of Washington. Continually examining my questions and how they were situated within the literature was a comforting process, as it made sense of events that were often emotional or upsetting. It was also useful to have such a large corpus of varying data to help inform or challenge these theories, constantly testing my understanding of both the literature and the young people I studied. At the same time, the sheer amount of data could be overwhelming in terms of keeping up with the transcription, analysis, and writing. We used various forms of technology, recording, and data-tracking systems to keep up with our developing impressions of the case study students and the contexts. Still, as Lareau puts it, "Like a greedy child on Christmas Day who keeps opening package after package without stopping to play with them and then asks for more, I kept going to the field, didn't write it up, but went back to the field anyway for fear of missing something really important" (p. 218). Discovering increasingly more about the students' experiences became addictive, and it was often tempting to observe without taking care to document our thoughts and interpretations. After a few visits where we were too caught up in their stories to take detailed notes, we found what we should have known all along—that a lack of documentation was actually detrimental to communicating the stories we cared so much about.

Moving Across Contexts

With all of the advantages cross-context research allows, it also came with its share of difficulties. First was scheduling. It was challenging enough to make sure I was dividing my time equally among the three settings, let alone coordinate my efforts with the rest of the team. It was frustrating when I could not be as consistent as I wanted about the regularity of our visits or when I had to delay important home visits because of scheduling issues. I also underestimated how hard it would be to balance data collection with disseminating the research at conferences, including the travel involved. I often wanted students to choose which classrooms we observed, but, unfortunately, scheduling multiple observations did not always allow this to work.

While scheduling was difficult and overwhelming, it was ultimately valuable to step back and redefine my analytic framework whenever I felt like I was losing sight of my questions. Playing such a continuous role in the lives of these students contributed to my understanding of what was important to them. This was especially apparent during the home visits, when I encountered students like James, who we initially thought was disinterested in science but turned out to be deeply involved at a leadership level, in his outdoor nature program. Or with Anthony, observing him at home, as I sat intimidated at the dinner table, listening to his stories of combat, challenged my initial assumption that he was exaggerating about his father's military career.

These cross-context observations allowed me to redefine my framework and ask questions that were more accurate in terms of the students' actual lives. While I initially wanted to compare in-school and out-of-school experiences, I know now that the divide is not all that clear. I also had to put aside my notion that all students viewed their disability label in a negative light or that they all disliked school. Reframing my questions in terms of learning environments allowed me to consider school as not one single context, but multiple learning environments that could all elicit different reactions from students. My initial frameworks were often too focused on the individual rather than on the activity contexts themselves, and also portrayed a model of the process of positioning that was too rigid for the fluid nature of human interaction and individual agency. My questions were continuously emerging, and working with a team helped me improve on my understandings of the connections between theory and practice.

Ethnographic Change and Privileging Youth Voice

As I have already reflected, one of the biggest struggles in studying ability across contexts was how I could maintain methodological rigor and consistency while also listening and adapting to students' stories in different places.

Part of the methodological rigor took place in the use of extensive "member checks," where we would show the case students drafts of papers and chapters involving their lives. This was useful in several cases to make sure I was accurately portraying and interpreting their experiences, but it was also difficult in terms of describing their relationship with disability (especially for Mark, who identified as no longer having a disability). What took me a long time to realize was that no matter what steps we took to ensure a certain level of objectivity, the actions and perceptions of any ethnographer inevitably become part of the contextual relations that influence youth participation. If relationships are a key part of challenging deficit orientations about ability, then the fact that I was building relationships with young people to privilege their voices and experiences was not inconsequential. Simply by having conversations about what they were experiencing in schools and in other contexts in their lives, I was providing them with an opportunity to reflect on their experiences that they might not have had. However much I tried to maintain my distance as a researcher, the ethnographer is always a part of the story. In light of the arguments already made about how youth with disabilities often are positioned in restrictive ways, being asked to be a part of the study inherently positioned them as individuals whose perspectives were valued. With relationships comes responsibility, and yet another tension I faced was how I could observe and engage with the students and not fulfill a moral responsibility to them when I witnessed instances that could have a lasting negative effect on their lives. After much discussion, the informal practice that the team and I adopted was not to intervene directly on behalf of a student unless explicitly requested to or unless the harm was particularly significant. The difficulty with enforcing such a rule was that it did not recognize that relationships and conversations themselves actually can be interventions. This was especially the case at Hillside, when I subconsciously used what I learned from the students during in the year to improve instruction at the summer program. The question that arose here was, is it ever appropriate (even in the case of a research study) to ignore lessons from students if it can improve their learning experience?

What I discovered from this experience was that after it was all over, I would still catch myself falling back into old patterns of getting caught up in my own busyness and not taking the time to ask students questions and collect as much detail about their lives as possible. I continued working with the Hillside debate team, but occasionally would catch myself becoming preoccupied with their success as competitors and spending less time focusing on them as people. Once I did not have the explicit requirement to go through the methods of focusing on the development of their abilities and identities, their unique selves began to fade away. The realization stunned me—how could I fall into the very same patterns I was advocating against? I sought to combat this disturbing development through the writing process, which I approached via a method that Gergen (2007) describes as "relational writing." Given the central role of human relationships in both the methodology and the findings themselves, writing in a way that highlighted key relationships and hopefully made them come alive seemed most appropriate. Although sections of the book have taken a more distanced, academic approach, I consciously made sure that the active nature of their lives could shine through. The interludes served as what Van Maanen (1988) terms "impressionist tales," which provide a glimpse into their human experiences.

The process of writing this book has reminded me once again about how ethnography, as unwieldy and complex as it can become, can act as a model for real life. The methods remind us of the importance of collecting stories, asking deep and challenging questions, questioning our own positionality and assumptions, and simply appreciating the intricate dynamics of people and their lives. A lack of time is an easy excuse for getting by on superficial, cursory information, the kind that one gets from asking, "How are you?" and continuing to walk on without hearing the answer. It is a short leap from settling for surface-level responses to making generalizations and relying on the "pictures in our minds" when making assumptions about people. The depth and richness of the fabric of human biographies warrants more time and careful treatment as well as concerted effort to build strong human relationships. As I discovered in the course of writing about the young people in this book, the rewards are well worthwhile—once I became a part of their story, they became a part of mine, and that is the kind of change that lasts forever.

References

Aronson, E., & Patnoe, S. (2011). *The jigsaw classroom: Building cooperation in the classroom* (2nd ed.). New York, NY: Addison Wesley Longman.

Aronson, J., Fried, C. B., & Good, C. (2002). Reducing the effects of stereotype threat on African-American college students by reshaping theories of intelligence. *Journal of Experimental School Psychology, 38,* 113–125.

Aronson, J., & Inzlicht, M. (2004). The ups and downs of attributional ambiguity: Stereotype vulnerability and the academic self-knowledge of African-American college students. *Psychological Science, 15,* 829–836.

Aronson, J., & Steele, C. M. (2005). Stereotypes and the fragility of human competence, motivation, and self-concept. In C. Dweck & E. Elliot (Eds.), *Handbook of competence and motivation* (pp. 436–456). New York, NY: Guilford.

Bagatell, N. (2003). *Constructing identities in social worlds: Stories from four adults with autism* (Unpublished doctoral dissertation). University of Southern California, Los Angeles.

Bagatell, N. (2007). Orchestrating voices: Autism, identity, and the power of discourse. *Disability & Society, 22*(4), 413–426.

Baines, A. D. (2011). Identities in motion: An ethnographic study of disability labels, social categories, and the everyday lives of youth (Doctoral dissertation). University of Washington, Seattle.

Baines, A. D. (2012). Positioning, strategizing, and charming: How students with autism construct identities in relation to disability. *Disability & Society, 27*(4), 547–561.

Bandura, A. (1986). *Social foundations of thought and action: A social cognitive theory.* Englewood Cliffs, NJ: Prentice-Hall.

Bandura, A. (1991). Self-regulation of motivation through anticipatory and self-reactive mechanisms. In R. A. Dienstbier (Ed.), *Perspectives on motivation: Nebraska Symposium on Motivation* (Vol. 38, pp. 69–164). Lincoln: University of Nebraska Press.

Bandura, A. (2001). Social cognitive theory: An agentic perspective. *Annual Review of Psychology, 52,* 1–26.

Baron-Cohen, S. (1993). Are children with autism acultural? *Behavioral and Brain Sciences, 16*(3), 512–513.

Barron, J., & Barron, S. (1992). *There's a boy in there.* New York, NY: Simon & Schuster.

Baumeister, R., & Leary, M. R. (1995). The need to belong: Desire for interpersonal attachments as a fundamental human motivation. *Psychological Bulletin, 117*(3), 497–529.

Biklen, D. (2005). *Autism and the myth of the person alone.* New York, NY: New York University Press.

Blackorby, J., & Cameto, R. (2004). Changes in school engagement and academic performance of students with disabilities. In *Wave 1 Wave 2 Overview* (SEELS) (pp. 8.1–8.23). Menlo Park, CA: SRI International.

Branfield, F. (1999). The disability movement: A movement of disabled people—a response to Paul S. Duckett. *Disability & Society, 14*(3), 399–403.

Brophy, J. E., & Good, T. (1974). *Teacher-child dyadic relationships: Causes and consequences.* New York, NY: Holt, Rinehart & Winston.

Burchardt, T. (2004). Capabilities of disability: The capabilities framework and the social model of disability. *Disability & Society, 19*(7), 735–751.

Burden, R. (2008). Is dyslexia necessarily associated with negative feelings of self-worth? A review and implications for future research. *Dyslexia, 14,* 188–196.

Campbell, J, & Oliver, M. (1996). *Disability politics: Understanding our past, changing our future.* London, England: Routledge.

Chang, D. F., & Demyan, A. (2007). Teachers' stereotypes of Asian, Black, and White students. *School Psychology Quarterly, 22,* 91–114.

Collins, K. M. (2013). *Ability profiling and school failure: One child's struggle to be seen as competent.* New York, NY: Routledge.

Conklin, H. C. (1964). Ethnogenealogical method. In W. H. Goodenough (Ed.), *Explorations in cultural anthropology: Essays in honor of George Peter Murdock* (pp. 25–55). New York, NY: McGraw-Hill.

Cooley, S. (1995). *Suspension/expulsion of regular and special education students in Kansas: A report to the Kansas State Board of Education.* Topeka: Kansas State Board of Education.

Cory, R. C. (2005). Identity, support and disclosure: Issues facing university students with invisible disabilities (Doctoral dissertation). Syracuse University, Syracuse, NY.

Cousin, P. T., Diaz, E., Flores, B., & Hernandez, J. (1995). Looking forward: Using a sociocultural perspective to reframe the study of learning disabilities. *Journal of Learning Disabilities, 28*(10), 656–663.

Coutinho, M. J., Oswald, D. P., & Best, A. M. (2002). The influence of sociodemographics and gender on the disproportionate identification of minority students as having learning disabilities. *Remedial and Special Education, 23,* 49–59.

Coutinho, M. J., Oswald, D. P., & Best, A. (2005). State variation in gender disproportionality in special education: Findings and recommendations. *Remedial and Special Education, 26,* 7–15.

Darling, R. B. (2003). Toward a model of changing disability identities: A proposed typology and research agenda. *Disability & Society, 18*(7), 881–895.

Davies, C. A., & Jenkins, R. (1997). "She has a different fits to me": How people with learning difficulties see themselves. *Disability & Society, 12*(1), 95–109.

Davis, J. E. (2001). Black boys at school: Negotiating masculinities and race. In R. Majors (Ed.), *Educating our Black children: New directions and radical approaches* (pp. 169–182). London, England: Routledge.

Diamond, M. C. (1988). *Enriching heredity.* New York, NY: Free Press.

Dreier, O. (2002). Personal trajectories of participation across contexts of social practice. *Outlines: Critical Social Studies, 1,* 5–32.

Dreier, O. (2009). Persons in structures of social practice. *Theory & Psychology, 19*(2), 193–212.

Dudley-Marling, C. (2004). The social construction of learning disabilities. *Journal of Learning Disabilities, 37*(6), 482–489.

Dweck, C. S. (1999). *Self-theories: Their role in motivation, personality and development.* Philadelphia, PA: Taylor & Francis.

Dweck, C. (2006). *Mindset.* New York, NY: Random House.

Dyson, M. E. (1994). Essentialism and the complexities of racial identity. In D. T. Goldberg (Ed.), *Multiculturalism: A critical reader* (pp. 218–229). Cambridge, MA: Blackwell.

Edgerton, R. B. (1993). *The cloak of competence.* Berkeley, CA: University of California Press.

Emerson, R. M., Fretz, R. I., & Shaw, L. L. (1995). *Writing ethnographic fieldnotes.* Chicago, IL: University of Chicago Press.

Emerson, R. M., & Pollner, M. (2001). Constructing participant/observation relations. In R. M. Emerson (Ed.), *Contemporary field research: Perspectives and formulations* (2nd ed., pp. 239–259). Prospect Heights, IL: Waveland Press.

Erickson, K., & Stull, D. (1998). *Doing team ethnography: Warnings and advice.* Thousand Oaks, CA: Sage.

Faulkner, W. (1950). *Requiem for a nun.* New York, NY: Vintage.

Feather, N. T. (Ed.). (1982). *Expectations and actions: Expectancy-value models in psychology.* Hillsdale, NJ: Erlbaum.

Ferguson, R. (2000). *A diagnostic analysis of Black–White GPA disparities in Shaker Heights, Ohio.* Washington, DC: Brookings Institution.

Ferri, B. A., & Connor, D. J. (2007). *Reading resistance: Discourses of exclusion in desegregation and inclusion debates.* New York, NY: Peter Lang.

Finkelstein, V. (1980). *Attitudes and disabled people: Issues for discussion.* New York, NY: World Rehabilitation Fund.

Fischer, F., & Forester, J. (Eds.). (1993). *The argumentative turn in policy analysis and planning.* Durham, NC: Duke University Press.

Fordham, S., & Ogbu, J. (1986). Black students' school success: Coping with the "burden of acting White." *Urban Review, 18,* 176–206.

Gabel, S., & Peters, S. (2004). Presage of a paradigm shift? Beyond the social model of disability toward resistance theories of disability. *Disability & Society, 19*(6), 585–600.

Gallego, M. A., Durán, G. Z., & Reyes, E. I. (2006). It depends: A sociohistorical account of the definition and methods of identification of learning disabilities. *Teachers College Record, 108*(11), 2195–2219.

Gardner, H. (1983). *Frames of mind.* New York, NY: Basic Books.

Geertz, C. (1973). Thick description: Toward an interpretive theory of culture. In *The interpretation of cultures* (pp. 4–30). New York, NY: Basic Books.

Gergen, K. J. (2007). Writing and relationship in academic culture. In M. Zachry & C. Thralls (Eds.), *Communicative practices in workplaces and the professions: Cultural perspectives on the regulation of discourse and organizations.* Amityville, NY: Baywood.

Goffman, E. (1959). *The presentation of self in everyday life.* Garden City, NY: Doubleday Anchor Books.

Grandin, T. (1992). An inside view of autism. In E. Schopler & G. B. Mesibov (Eds.), *High-functioning individuals with autism.* New York, NY: Plenum Press.

Gregory, J. F. (1996). The crime of punishment: Racial and gender disparities in the use of corporal punishment in the U.S. public schools. *Journal of Negro Education, 64,* 454–462.

Griffin, B. W. (2002). Academic disidentification, race, and high school dropouts. *High School Journal, 85*(4), 71–81.

Hapner, A., & Imel, B. (2002). The students' voices: "Teachers started to listen and show respect." *Remedial and Special Education, 23*(2), 122–126.

Harpur, P. (2012). From disability to ability: Changing the phrasing of the debate. *Disability & Society, 27*(3), 325–337.

Harré, R. (1983). *Personal being: A theory for individual psychology.* Oxford, England: Basil Blackwell.

Harré, R. (2008). Positioning theory. *Self-Care and Dependent Care Nursing, 16*(1), 28–32.

Harré, R. & Moghaddam, F. (Eds.). (2003). *The self and others: Positioning individuals and groups in personal, political, and cultural contexts.* Westport, CT: Praeger.

Harré, R., Moghaddam, F. M., Cairnie, T. P., Rothbart, D., & Sabat, S. R. (2009). Recent advances in positioning theory. *Theory & Psychology, 19*(1), p. 5–31.

Harré, R., & Slocum, N. (2003). Disputes as complex social events: On the uses of positioning theory. In R. Harré & F. Moghaddam (Eds.), *The self and others: Positioning individuals and groups in personal, political, and cultural contexts* (pp. 123–136). Westport, CT: Praeger.

Harré, R., & VanLangenove, L. (Eds.) (1999). *Positioning theory: Moral contexts of intentional action.* Malden, MA: Blackwell.

Harry, B., Klingner, J. K., Sturges, K. M., & Moore, R. F. (2005). Of Rocks and Soft Places: Using qualitative methods to investigate disproportionality. In D. J. Losen & G. Orfield (Eds.), *Racial Inequity in Special Education* (pp. 71–92). Cambridge, MA: Harvard Education Press.

Harry, B., & Klingner, J. K. (2006). *Why are so many minority students in special education? Understanding race and disability in schools.* New York, NY: Teachers College Press.

Harry, B., Klingner, J., & Cramer, E. (2007). *Case studies of minority student placement in special education.* New York, NY: Teachers College Press.

Heath, S. B., & McLaughlin, M. W. (Eds.). (1993). *Identity and inner-city youth: Beyond ethnicity and gender.* New York, NY: Teachers College Press.

Hehir, T. (2005). *New directions in special education: Eliminating ableism in policy and practice.* Cambridge, MA: Harvard University Press.

Henry, J. (1963). *Culture against man.* New York, NY: Vintage Books.

Herring, S. C. (2007). Questioning the Generational Divide: Technological exoticism and adult constructions of online youth identity. In D. Buckingham (Ed.), *Youth, Identity, and Digital Media* (pp. 71–92). Cambridge, MA: The MIT Press.

Higgins, E. L., Raskind, M. H., Goldberg, R. J., & Herman, K. L. (2002). Stages of acceptance of a learning disability: The impact of labeling. *Learning Disability Quarterly, 25,* 3–18.

Hilliard, A. (1991). Do we have the will to educate all children? *Educational Leadership, 49*(1), 31–36.

Holland, D., Lachicotte, W., Jr., Skinner, D., & Cain, C. (1998). *Identity and agency in cultural worlds.* Cambridge, MA: Harvard University Press.

Holland, D., & Lave, J. (2001). *History in person: Enduring struggles, contentious practice, intimate identities.* Santa Fe, NM: School of American Research Press.

Holland, D., & Leander, K. (2004). Ethnographic studies of positioning and subjectivity: An introduction. *Ethos, 32*(2),127–139.

Illich, I. (1971). *Deschooling society.* London, England: Harper & Row.

Imich, A. J. (1994). Exclusions from school: Current trends and issues. *Educational Research, 36*(1), 3–11.

Inden, R. (1990). *Imagining India.* Oxford, England: Blackwell.

Jack, J. (2011). "The Extreme Male Brain?" Incrementum and the rhetorical gendering of autism. *Disability Studies Quarterly, 31*(3). Retrieved from http://dsq-sds.org/article/view/1672/1599

Keefe, E. B., Moore, V. M., & Duff, F. R. (2006). *Listening to the experts: Students with disabilities speak out.* Baltimore, MD: Paul H. Brookes.

Kegan, R. (2001). Easing a world of pain: Learning disabilities and the psychology of self-understanding. In P. Rodis, A. Garrod, & M. L. Boscardin (Eds.), *Learning disabilities and life stories* (pp. 194–204). Needham Heights, MA: Allyn & Bacon.

Kellam, S. G., Ling, X., Merisca, R., Brown, C. H., & Ialongo, N. (1998). The effect of the level of aggression in the first grade classroom on the course and malleability of aggressive behavior into middle school. *Development and Psychopathology, 10,* 165–185.

Kelly, B. (2005). "Chocolate . . . makes you autism": Impairment, disability and childhood identities. *Disability & Society, 20*(3), 261–275.

Kistner, J., Metzler, A., Gatlin, D., & Risi, S. (1993). Classroom racial proportions and children's peer relations: Race and gender effects. *Journal of Educational Psychology, 85,* 446–452.

Kolb, B., & Whishaw, I. Q. (1998). Brain plasticity and behavior. *Annual Review of Psychology, 49,* 43–64.

Knox, J. E., & Stevens, C. (1993). Vygotsky and Soviet Russian defectology: An introduction. In L. S. Vygotsky, *The collected works of L. S. Vygotsky: Vol. 2. The fundamentals of defectology* (pp. 1–25). New York, NY: Springer.

Kuipers, J., & McDermott, R. P. (Eds.). (2007). *Fine description: Ethnographic and linguistic essays by Harold C. Conklin* (Yale University Southeast Asia Studies, Monograph 56). New Haven, CT: Yale University Press.

Lareau, A. (1996). Common problems in field work: A personal essay. In A. Lareau & J. Shultz (Eds.), *Journeys through ethnography: Realistic accounts of fieldwork* (pp. 195–236). Boulder, CO: Westview Press.

Lave, J. (1987). *Cognition in practice.* New York, NY: Cambridge University Press.

Lave, J., & Wenger, E. (1991). *Situated learning: Legitimate peripheral participation.* Cambridge, England: Cambridge University Press.

Lemke, J. I. (2000). Across the scales of time: Artifacts, activities, and meanings in ecosocial systems. *Mind, Culture, and Activity, 7*(4), 273–290.

Locke, E. A., & Latham, G. P. (1990). *A theory of goal setting and task performance.* Englewood Cliffs, NJ: Prentice-Hall.

Losen, D. J., & Orfield, G. (Eds.). (2005). *Racial inequity in special education*. Cambridge, MA: Harvard University Press.

Madison, D. S. (2005). *Critical Ethnography: Method, ethics, and performance*. Thousand Oaks, CA: Sage Publications.

Matthews, C. K., & Harrington, N. G. (2000). Invisible disability. In D. O Braithwaite & T. L Thompson (Eds.), *Handbook of communication and people with disabilities: Research and application* (pp. 405–421). Mahwah, NJ: Erlbaum.

McAdams, D. (1997). The case for unity of the (post) modern self: A modest proposal. In R. D. Ashmore & L. Jussim (Eds.), *Self and identity: Fundamental issues* (pp. 46–78). New York, NY: Oxford University Press.

McDermott, R. (1993). The acquisition of a child by a learning disability. In S. Chaiklin & J. Lave (Eds.), *Understanding practice: Perspectives on activity and context* (pp. 269 –305). New York, NY: Cambridge University Press.

McDermott, R., Goldman, S., & Varenne, H. (2006). The cultural work of learning disabilities. *Educational Researcher, 35*(6), 12–17.

McDermott, R., & Varenne, H. (1996). Culture as disability. *Anthropology & Education Quarterly, 26*(3), 324–348.

McKown, C., & Weinstein, R. S. (2003). The development and consequences of stereotype-consciousness in middle childhood. *Child Development, 74*(2), 498–515.

Mehan, H. (1996). The construction of an LD student. In M. Silverstein & G. Urban (Eds.), *Natural histories of discourse* (pp. 253–276). Chicago, IL: University of Chicago Press.

Mehan, H. (2008). A sociological perspective on opportunity to learn and assessment. In P. A. Moss, D. C. Pullin, J. P. Gee, E. H. Haertel, & L. J. Young (Eds.), *Assessment, equity, and opportunity to learn* (pp. 42–75). Cambridge, England: Cambridge University Press.

Meier, K., Stewart, J., & England, R. (1989). *Race, class and education: The politics of second generation discrimination*. Madison, WI: University of Wisconsin Press.

Molloy, H., & Vasil, L. (2002). The social construction of Asperger syndrome: The pathologizing of difference? *Disability & Society, 17*(6), 659–669.

Mooney, J. (2007). *The short bus: A journey beyond normal*. New York, NY: Holt Paperbacks.

Morrison, T. (2007). *The Bluest Eye*. New York, NY: Vintage International.

Nakkula, M. (2008). Identity and possibility: Adolescent development and the potential of schools. In M. Sadowski (Ed.), *Adolescents at school: Perspectives on youth, identity, and education* (pp. 11–21). Cambridge, MA: Harvard Education Press.

Nakkula, M., & Ravitch, S. (1998). *Matters of interpretation: Reciprocal transformation in therapeutic and developmental relationships with youth*. San Francisco, CA: Jossey-Bass.

Nasir, N. S., & Cooks, J. (2009). Becoming a hurdler: How learning settings afford identities. *Anthropology & Education Quarterly, 40*(1), 41–61.

Nasir, N. S., & Hand, V. (2008). From the court to the classroom: Opportunities for engagement, learning, and identity in basketball and classroom mathematics. *The Journal of the Learning Sciences, 17,* 143–179.

National Research Council. (2002). *Minority students in special and gifted education* (M. Donovan & C. Cross, Eds.). Washington, DC: National Academies Press.

Noguera, P. A. (2003). The trouble with Black boys: The role and influence of environmental and cultural factors on the academic performance of African-American males. *Urban Education, 38*(4), 431–459.

Oakes, J. (2005). *Keeping track: How schools structure inequality.* New Haven, CT: Yale University Press.

Oliver, M., & Barnes, C. (1998). *Disabled people and social policy: From exclusion to inclusion.* London, England: Longman.

Olney, M. F., & Brockelman, K. F. (2003). Out of the disability closet: Strategic use of perception management by select university students with disabilities. *Disability & Society, 18*(1), 35–50.

Olson, K. (2009). *Wounded by school: Recapturing the joy in learning and standing up to old school culture.* New York, NY: Teachers College Press.

Oppenheim, R. (1974). *Effective teaching methods for autistic children.* Springfield, IL: Thomas.

Pea, R., & Brown, J. S. (1991). Foreword In J. Lave & E. Wenger, *Situated learning: Legitimate peripheral participation* (pp. 11–13). Cambridge, England: Cambridge University Press.

Penuel, W. R., & Wertsch, J. V. (1995). Vygotsky and identity formation: A sociocultural approach. *Educational Psychologist, 30*(2), 83–92.

Peters, S. (2000). Is there a disability culture? A syncretisation of three possible world views. *Disability & Society, 15*(4), 583–601.

Phelan, P., Davidson, A. L., & Cao, H. T. (1991). Students' multiple worlds: Negotiating the boundaries of family, peer, and school cultures. *Anthropology & Education Quarterly, 22*(3), 224–250.

Phelan, P., Davidson, A. L., & Yu, H. C. (1998). *Adolescents' Worlds: Negotiating family, peers, and school.* New York, NY: Teachers College Press.

Plath, D. W. (1980). *Long engagements: Maturity in modern Japan.* Stanford, CA: Stanford University Press.

Pope, D. C. (2001). *"Doing school": How we are creating a generation of stressed out, materialistic, and miseducated students.* New Haven, CT: Yale University Press.

Postman, N. (1988). *Conscientious objections.* New York, NY: Knopf.

Purdie-Vaughns, V., & Eibach, R. B. (2008). Intersectional invisibility: The distinctive advantages and disadvantages of multiple subordinate group identities. *Sex Roles, 59,* 377–391.

Rabiee, P., & Glendinning, C. (2010). Choice: What, when, and why? Exploring the importance of choice to disabled people. *Disability & Society, 25*(7), 827–839.

Raible, J., & Nieto, S. (2008). Beyond categories: The complex identities of adolescents. In M. Sadowski (Ed.), *Adolescents at school: Perspectives on youth, identity, and education* (pp. 207–223). Cambridge, MA: Harvard Education Press.

Rapley, M. (2004). *The social construction of intellectual disability.* Cambridge, England: Cambridge University Press.

Reid, D. K., & Valle, J. W. (2004). The discursive practice of learning disability: Implications for instruction and parent–school relations [Special series]. *Journal of Learning Disabilities, 37*(6), 466–481.

Rodis, P., Garrod, A., & Boscardin, M. L. (2001). *Learning disabilities & life stories.* Needham Heights, MA: Allyn & Bacon.

Rong, X. L. (1996). Effects of race and gender on teachers' perceptions of the social behavior of elementary students. *Urban Education, 31,* 261–290.

Rose, D. H., & Meyer, A. (2002). *Teaching every student in the digital age: Universal design for learning.* Alexandria, VA: ASCD.

Rose, D. H., & Meyer, A. (2006). *A practical reader in universal design for learning.* Cambridge, MA: Harvard Education Press.

Rose, D. H., Meyer, A., & Hitchcock, C. (2005). *The universally designed classroom: Accessible curriculum and digital technologies.* Cambridge, MA: Harvard Education Press.

Sadowski, M. (Ed.). (2008). *Adolescents at school: Perspectives on youth, identity, and education.* Cambridge, MA: Harvard Education Press.

Sarason, S. B. (1990). *The challenge of art to psychology.* New Haven, CT: Yale University Press.

Sen, A. (1992). *Inequality reexamined.* Oxford, England: Oxford University Press.

Sen, A. (1999). *Development as freedom.* Oxford, England: Oxford University Press.

Shakespeare, T. (1996). Disability, identity, and difference. In C. Barnes & G. Mercer (Eds.), *Exploring the divide* (pp. 94–113). Leeds, England: The Disability Press.

Shakespeare, T., & Watson, N. (2002). The social model of disability: An outdated ideology? *Research in Social Science and Disability, 12,* 9–28.

Shapiro, J. P. (1994). *No pity: People with disabilities forging a new civil rights movement.* New York, NY: Three Rivers Press.

Skiba, R. J., Michael, R. S., Nardo, A. C., & Peterson, R. L. (2002). The Color of Discipline: Sources of racial and gender disproportionality in school punishment. *The Urban Review, 34*(4), 317-342.

Slaughter-Defoe, D. T., & Richards, H. (1994). Literacy as empowerment: The case for African-American males. In V. L. Gadsden & D. A. Wagner (Eds.), *Literacy among African-American youth: Issues in learning, teaching, and schooling* (pp. 125–147). Cresskill, NJ: Hampton Press.

Slocum, N., & Van Langenhove, L. (2003). Integration speak: Introducing positioning theory in regional integration studies. In R. Harré (Ed.), *The self and others: Positioning individuals and groups in personal, political, and cultural contexts* (pp.219 –234). Westport, CT: Praeger.

Smith, J. D. (2007). Mental retardation and the problem of "normality": Self-determination and identity choice. *Education and Training in Developmental Disabilities, 42*(4), 410–417.

Specht, J. A., Polgar, J. M., Willoughby, C., King, G., & Brown, E. (2000). A retrospective look at the educational experiences of individuals with disabilities. *Exceptionality Education Canada, 10(3),* 25–39.

Steele, C. M. (1997). A threat in the air: How stereotypes shape intellectual identity and performance. *American Psychologist, 52,* 613–629.

Steele, C. M. (2010). *Whistling Vivaldi and other clues to how stereotypes affect us.* New York, NY: Norton.

Steinberg, L. (1996). *Beyond the classroom: Why school reform has failed and what parents need to do.* New York, NY: Simon & Schuster.

Swain, J., & French, S. (2000). Towards an affirmation model of disability. *Disability & Society, 15*(4), 569–582.

Tatum, B. D. (1997). *Why are all the Black kids sitting together in the cafeteria?* New York, NY: Basic Books.

Terzi, L. (2005). A capability perspective on impairment, disability, and special needs: Towards social justice in education. *Theory and Research in Education, 3*(2), 197–223.

Timimi, S. (2011). Autism is not a scientifically valid or clinically useful diagnosis. *BMJ*, 343. doi: http://dx.doi.org/10.1136/bmj.d5105

Tyson, K. (2003). Notes from the back of the room: Problems and paradoxes in the schooling of young Black students. *Sociology of Education, 76*(4), 326–343.

Vadeboncoeur, J. A., & Portes, P. R. (2002). Students "at risk": Exploring identity from a sociocultural perspective. In D. McInerney & S. V. Etten (Eds.), *Sociocultural influences on motivation and learning* (pp. 89–128). Greenwich, CT: Information Age.

Van Maanen, J. (1988). *Tales of the field: On writing ethnography*. Chicago, IL: University of Chicago Press.

Varenne, H., & McDermott, R. P. (1998). *Successful failure: The school America builds*. Boulder, CO: Westview Press.

Vygotsky, L. S. (1993). *The collected works of L. S. Vygotsky: Vol. 2. The fundamentals of defectology*. New York, NY: Springer.

Walford, G. (2008). The nature of educational ethnography. In G. Walford (Ed.), *How to do educational ethnography* (pp. 1–15). London, England: The Tufnell Press.

Watson, N. (2002). Well, I know this is going to sound very strange to you, but I don't see myself as a disabled person: Identity and disability. *Disability & Society, 17*(5), 509–527.

Wehmeyer, M. L. (2008). The impact of disability on adolescent identity. In M. Sadowski (Ed.), *Adolescents at school: Perspectives on youth, identity, and education* (pp. 167–179). Cambridge, MA: Harvard Education Press.

Weinstein, R. S. (2002). *Reaching higher: The power of expectations in schooling*. Cambridge, MA: Harvard University Press.

Wenger, E. (1998). *Communities of practice: Learning, meaning, and identity*. New York, NY: Cambridge University Press.

Willis, P., & Trondman, M. (2000). Manifesto for ethnography. *Ethnography, 1*(5), 5–16.

Wolcott, H. F. (1997). Ethnographic research in education. In R. M. Jaeger (Ed.), *Complementary methods for research in education* (2nd ed., pp. 327–364). Washington, DC: American Educational Research Association.

Wortham, S. (2004). From good student to outcast: The emergence of a classroom identity. *Ethos, 32*(2), 164–187.

Wortham, S. (2006). *Learning identity: The joint emergence of social identification and academic learning*. New York, NY: Cambridge University Press.

Wortham, S. (2008). The objectification of identity across events. *Linguistics and Education, 19*(3), 294–311.

Index

About the Author

AnnMarie D. Baines is an assistant professor in the Department of Secondary Education at San Francisco State University. She is broadly interested in the social construction of disability, academic identity development, and perceptions and beliefs about intelligence, inclusion, and learning across settings. Her work follows youth in school and after-school contexts to study how everyday interactions and institutional histories shape student learning, academic identity, and adolescent development. As a consultant, she focuses on approaches to universally design learning environments to promote access and support for all learners. At San Francisco State, she teaches courses in Adolescent Development and Inclusive Education, in addition to supervising preservice secondary teachers. Current projects include universally designing middle schools, improving school connectedness for high school youth, writing on the culture of poverty, and working with the West Contra Costa Unified School District.

As an ethnographer, her past research focused on high school classrooms, debate teams, music groups, and informal science settings. During her time as a graduate researcher for the Learning in Informal and Formal Environments (LIFE) Center, she completed studies of inclusion in high school debate, a Gates Foundation curriculum project incorporating Universal Design for Learning, and a National Science Foundation–funded, cross-setting ethnography of high school students with social and learning disabilities. In addition to her academic work, Baines has been a debate coach for 12 years, taught high school special education in the Boston Public Schools, and received her teaching credential through the Boston Teacher Residency Program. Baines has a master's degree in Education Policy and Management from Harvard Graduate School of Education and majored in political science at University of California, Berkeley. She received her PhD in Educational Psychology and the Learning Sciences from the University of Washington, where she was awarded a Presidential Fellowship from the Graduate Opportunities and Minority Achievement Program. More details on her work can be found at www.adbaines.com